THE CROWNING OF HIS WORK

THE CROWNING OF HIS WORK

Paul Sédir

FRIENDS IN SPIRIT

First published in French as
Le Couronnement de l'oeuvre
A.-L. Legrand, Éditeur
Sotteville-lez-Rouen, 1926
First English edition © Friends in Spirit, 2024
an imprint of Sophia Perennis
Translation © Friends in Spirit 2024
Series Editor: James R. Wetmore

All rights reserved

No part of this book may be reproduced or transmitted,
in any form or by any means, without permission

For information, address:
Friends in Spirit
Box 931, Philmont, NY 12565

ISBN 978-1-59731-225-7 (pbk)
ISBN 978-1-59731-226-4 (cloth)

Cover Design: Michael Schrauzer

CONTENTS

Biographical Sketch i

CHAPTER I
The Aspects of the Messiah 1

Christic Energy 18
The Civilizing Jesus 21
The Rear-Guard 23
What Jesus Is 25
Teratology 29
The Sheepfold 32
The Shepherd 35

CHAPTER II
The Just Judge 41

Pharisaism 59
The Three Binaries 62
The Whitened Sepulchers 65
The Sanctions 68
The Day and the Hour 75
Patience 80
The Mystical Judgment 88
The Sentence of the Judge 92

CHAPTER III
The Faithful Friend 97

The Victory of Ascendant Love 120
The Effort of Descendant Love 129
The Meeting of the Two Currents 138
This Meeting is a Being 146
Renunciation 152
Palm Sunday 158
The Rite of Union 162
Perenniality of Union 167
The Friends 172
Peace 175
The Testament of the Friend 178

CHAPTER IV
The Crowning of His Work 183

Redemption 216
The Garden of Olives 220
The Tribunals 224
The Crucifixion 230
Resurrection 236
The Apparitions 240
The Future 246
Recapitulation 251

Acknowledgments

The publisher is deeply indebted to the "friends" of *Les Amitiés Spirituelles*, who have kept Paul Sédir's books in print in French for over a century, and for the dedication of those who have nurtured the vision that one day these books might appear in worthy editions for Anglophone readers. We gratefully thank in this connection Piers Vaughn and Peter Urbanski for the exchange of textual materials many years ago that led to this presents series, Robert Ledwidge for his technical assistance, and especially Madame Zadah Guérin-McCaffery, who nurtured this same vision and worked towards its realization for decades. Her skilled devotion to Sédir's works helped ensure that Sédir's carefully crafted style has been preserved in these Friends in Spirit translations.

Biographical Sketch

HVON LE LOUP, son of Hippolyte Le Loup and Séraphine Foeller, was born on January 2, 1871 in Dinan, in the Côtes du Nord region of France. As a child, Yvon suffered the effects of tuberculosis, partial blindness, and a grave leg fracture that troubled him throughout his life. His mother, of Hessian origin, taught him German, which he later spoke fluently. At the age of nine, he made his First Communion at St Augustin's church, then entered the Jesuit school on rue des Francs Bourgeois, where he quickly distinguished himself by his great intelligence. Observant to a fault, he became a fine draughtsman and would have liked to paint. He was drawn to music, drawing, literature, and was extraordinarily dexterous with his hands. In due course, however, he was obliged to pursue a more practical academic course, owing to the influence of his father, an old soldier imbued with discipline who had little understanding for the refinement of this quiet child with lofty aspirations. And so, as soon a Yvon passed his academic exams (1892), he joined the Banque de France. He was twenty-one years old.

A few years earlier, in his late teens (around 1890), a profound shift in Yvon's orientation had taken shape. Not far from the Banque de France was an esoteric bookshop and publishing house (La Librairie du Merveilleux), where Yvon soon met the well-known writer on esoteric matters, Dr. Gerard Encausse (Papus). This led to a great friendship

i

THE CROWNING OF HIS WORK

between the two quite different men. Papus set the young Yvon to work organizing his extensive esoteric library and introduced him to numerous personalities from the heady, even feverish, esoteric milieu of the time. One evening, he was taken to the home of Stanislas de Guaita, a nobleman of Italian descent who possessed the most complete esoteric library then in existence. Around this time, Yvon published an article ("An Experiment in Practical Occultism") and made his debut as a speaker on the theme: "Divinatory Sciences and Chiromancy."

In 1891, Papus had formed the Order of Martinists, based on the teachings of "The Unknown Philosopher," Louis Claude de Saint-Martin (1743–1803), and asked Yvon to collaborate. This fraternity took up the ideas of Martinez de Pasqually's Kabbalistic rite, and formed the first initiatory level of Guaita's Rosicrucian fraternity. In these circles, young authors frequently used pseudonyms. Yvon took the name Paul Sédir (anagram of désir), Gerard Encausse became Papus, Dr. Emmanuel Lalande used the name Marc Haven, etc. From the time of his association with the new Martinist Order, Yvon regularly published his work as Paul Sédir.

In 1895, Papus passed his doctorate in medicine and opened a home for the aged. This necessitated Sédir taking on the bulk of the esoteric-hermetic activities on which he and Papus had been collaborating. Every evening he gave classes in Hebrew and Sanskrit, the psychic training of Hindu fakirs, yoga, experimental alchemy, astrology, esoteric botany, etc. He also organized various research groups on related subjects.

Sédir was also much attracted to mysticism, and frequented literary circles such that of the poet Paul-Marie

Biographical Sketch

Verlaine. Meanwhile, in the rue de l'Ancienne Comédie, meetings of the Martinist Order were taking place, where Sédir became acquainted with individuals engaged in experiments regarding which he would later say: "It is here-below that you pay the highest price." His alchemical research did, however, enable him to acquire an ever deeper understanding of the foundations of what is known as the Great Work.

All these early aspects of Sédir's esoteric life reveal an overarching quest for truth that always led him to first experience something before speaking about it. He had by now attained great heights of "secret" knowledge, and even power. But to his great good fortune he had the wisdom to detach himself from these as soon as he realized their worthlessness and danger.

⊕

In July 1897, Gerard Encausse arranged for Sédir (then 26 years old) to meet a most singular man, Master Philippe of Lyon (Nizier Anthelme Philippe), to whom he was introduced by Madame Encausse. Master Philippe was a remarkable healer whom Sédir and others in his circle considered a Christian Master of the highest degree. Shortly after this meeting, Sédir left for Lyon to spend his vacation there. Just what happened at that time remains a private matter, although Sédir gives some inkling of what transpired in his autobiographical book *Initiations*, and also in a remarkable letter of May 1910:

> Together with some companions, I have done the rounds of all esotericisms and explored all crypts with the most fervent sincerity and hope of success. But none of the certainties I eventually grasped appeared

THE CROWNING OF HIS WORK

to be The Certainty. Rabbis communicated their secret manuscripts to me; alchemists admitted me to their laboratories; Sufis, Buddhists, and Taoists led me during long nights to the abodes of their gods; a Brahmin let me copy his tables of mantra; a yogi imparted to me the secrets of contemplation. But one evening, after a certain meeting, what these admirable men taught became for me like haze rising at dusk on a sultry day. We run after what we think is hidden, but know nothing of our own religion, though its dogma and liturgy are the most complete presentation of integral knowledge on earth. Everything is there in Christianity. The Hindu *trimurti* is neither the Christian trinity nor the Pythagorean ternary; gnosis and the gospels do not lead to the same goal. Read in the texts what is there, not what one would wish to find there. To see that we know nothing; to experience that we can do nothing; to verify that heaven is here within us, and that our Friend constantly enfolds us within his blessed arms—this is the lesson of Jesus. This I have attempted to say by publishing, among other works, five volumes of lectures on the gospels.

Master Philippe had changed Sédir's orientation. *His mission had been affirmed.* He gave up all the esoteric fraternities (and his various ranks and offices in them) in order to devote himself wholly to living and spreading the gospel. His commentaries on the life of Christ are especially notable in that he accepts the intuitive faculty as a means of approaching the Truth. Sédir's literary output was extensive. His best known works are from this period are: *Prayer, Initiations, Mystic Forces, Christian Mysticism, Seven Mystical Gardens, The Childhood of Jesus, The Sermon on the Mount,*

Biographical Sketch

Some Friends of God, The Healings of Christ, The Kingdom of God, The Crowning of His Work, Weekly Meditations, and *The Incandescent Path*. His lectures and books drew many devoted students, and in due course a fellowship called Les Amitiés Spirituelles ("Friends in Spirit") was formed. This organization undertook to publish many of Sédir's books, and though it is much diminished, it remains active today.

Sédir died in Paris. Twenty years later, Breton poet and novelist Théophile Briant of Dinan wrote:

> On February 3, 1926, Paul Sédir died in Paris at the age of 55. The death of this admirable man, with his gospel-inspired heart, went almost unnoticed by the mainstream press, which was more preoccupied with crowning the charlatans and histrionics who were entertaining the public, even as international catastrophes were on the verge of breaking out. Apart from the chosen few whom this Apostle of the End Times had called to the Light, most post-war jabberers were unaware that one of the century's most eloquent voices was no longer to be heard. His was a forerunner's voice, the voice of a herald proclaiming in a wilderness of contentious crowds, a voice that had been devoted for years to spreading the gospel and, at the threshold of the abyss, was raised in dire warning against the multiplied prostitutions of the word.†

---

† This sketch is based on biographical materials provided by Émile Besson and Max Camis (close friends of Sédir), recently published in English in *Paul Sédir: His Life and Work* (Friends in Spirit, 2024).

CHAPTER I

The Aspects of the Messiah

Each chapter begins with a synoptic extract from the gospels that provides the subject matter for the subsections that follow.

N HIS WAY up to Jerusalem, Jesus particularly took the Twelve with him; and while walking along he told them: "We are now going to Jerusalem. All the things which the prophets have written about the Son of Man will be accomplished; the Son of Man shall be handed over to the head priests and to the scribes, who will condemn him to die; then they will deliver him to the pagans (Gentiles), that he may be jeered, scourged, and crucified; and on the third day, he will rise again." The disciples did not understand any of this; it was an impenetrable language that had no meaning for them.

Then the mother of the sons of Zebedee brought John and James to him; she knelt at his feet, to make a request. He asked her: "What do you want?" She answered him: "Order that in your kingdom my two sons who are here will be seated, one on your right and the other on your left." Jesus answered: "You know not what you are asking for. Can you drink the cup I must drink, or be baptized with the kind of baptism I must receive?" "That we can do," they replied. But he went on: "Yes, you will drink from my cup and you will receive the same baptism I am to receive; but as to sitting at my right or my left, it is not up to me to grant it; those places belong to those for whom my Father has prepared them." Upon learning this, the other ten were indignant against the two brothers. Then Jesus called them and told them: "You know that the princes rule and lord it over the nations, that the powerful vaunt their power over them. It shall not be so with

THE CROWNING OF HIS WORK

you; on the contrary, let him who wants to become great among you be your servant, and whoever wants to be the first among you be your slave, because the Son of Man did not come to be served, but to serve and to give his life as a ransom for the many."

As Jesus left Jericho, a great multitude followed him. There were two blind men seated along the road, who upon hearing that this was Jesus passing by, cried out: "Take pity on us, Lord, Son of David." The crowd menaced them to keep quiet, but they shouted still louder: "Take pity on us, Lord, Son of David!" Jesus stopped, called them over, asking: "What do you want me to do?" They answered: "Lord, let our eyes be opened!" Moved by compassion, Jesus touched their eyes. And suddenly, they recovered their sight and followed him.

After which, Jesus traveled throughout Galilee, not wanting to go through Judea, where the Jews were attempting to have him put to death. However, the Jewish feast known as of Tabernacles was approaching and his brothers told him: "Leave this particular country; travel to Judea so that your disciples also will see the works you are accomplishing. One does not act in secret when one wants to be known. Since you are doing these things, manifest yourself to the world." (In fact, his brothers did not believe in him either.) Jesus answered them: "My time has not yet come; as for you whom the world does not hate, the opportune moment is always there; but the world hates me because I bear testimony to its evil doings. Go to the feast; as for me, I am not attending that feast just yet,

The Aspects of the Messiah

because my time has not yet come."—This said, he remained in Galilee. Later, when his brothers had left for the feast, he too went, not overtly but rather secretly.

During the feast, however, the Jews were querying: "Who is he?" There was a lot of whispering about him among the crowd. "He is a good man," said a few. "No, said others, quite to the contrary, he leads the people astray." But no one, for fear of the Jews, dared express themselves openly.

The feast was half over, when Jesus went up to the Temple and began teaching. The Jews were astonished, saying: "How can this man be so well versed, he who has not studied?" Jesus answered them: "My teaching is not my own, it comes from him who sent me. If any one is prepared to do his will, he will know whether my learning comes from God or if I am giving a message of my own. The man who speaks from his own knowledge pursues his own glory, but he who pursues to glorify the One who sent him is veracious and without fraud. Was it not Moses who gave you the Law? Yet none of you keep the Law and not one of you puts it into practice! Why are you attempting to kill me?"

The crowd responded: "You are possessed by a demon. Who is trying to kill you?" Jesus replied with these words: "One of my actions (works) has astounded you all. Moses prescribed circumcision (it was not instituted by Moses, it comes from the Patriarchs); yet this circumcision you perform on the sabbath. Why are you irritated against me for having made a man whole on the sabbath? Do not judge according to appearances, but judge according to justice."

Some inhabitants of Jerusalem were saying: "Is this not the man they are attempting to put to death? Yet, here he is speaking openly, and no one chides him. Might it be that the rulers have recognized him as the Christ? We are well aware where this man came from; and when the Christ will come no one will know from whence."

Then Jesus teaching at the Temple cried out: "You know me and know whence I came! I did not come of my own accord, but the One who sent me is real and you know Him not; I, I know Him, because I came from Him and it is He who sent me." They were attempting to seize him; however no one put a hand on him because his time had not yet come. But among the people, several believed in him and were saying: "When the Christ will come, will he perform more miracles than this man does?" The Pharisees heard about the remarks that were currently uttered among the multitudes; so the chief sacrificers conspired with them to send agents to take hold of him and to arrest him.

Jesus then added: "I am still with you for a short while; later I shall go back to the One who sent me. You will look for me and you will not find me, because where I shall be you cannot come." The Jews were saying to each other: "Where is he going that we cannot find him? Is he going to those who are seated among the Greeks and teach the Greeks? What does it mean: 'You

The Aspects of the Messiah

will search for me and you will not find me, and then, where I shall be you cannot come?'"

On the last and greatest day of the feast, Jesus was there. He stood up and exclaimed: "If any one is thirsty, let him come to me and drink. From him who believes in me, as the Scriptures foretold, living water will flow from his heart." He was referring to the Holy Spirit that those who believed in him were to receive; for the Spirit had not yet been given because Jesus had not yet been glorified. Many people among the multitude, having heard these remarks said: "This man is truly the Prophet." Others said: "It is the Christ." Still others: "But will the Christ come from Galilee? Do not the Scriptures state that it is from the house of David that the Christ is to come?" However, the peoples were divided on the subject. A few among them wanted to grab him; but no one laid hands on him.

The officers (agents) then turned towards the principal sacrificers and Pharisees. These latter said: "Why haven't you brought him here?" The agents answered: "No one has ever spoken as this man does!" The Pharisees then told them: "Have you too been seduced? Is there one chief or one Pharisee that has believed in him, yet? And this rabble without knowledge of the Law is execrable." Nicodemus, the very one who had come to Jesus secretly and who was one of them, told them: "Does our Law permit to judge a man without having heard him, by first finding out what he is doing?" They answered: "Are you a Galilean, you too? Inform yourself and you will find out that no prophet comes from Galilee."

THE CROWNING OF HIS WORK

Jesus again went on speaking to them: "I am the light of the world. He who follows me will never walk in darkness but will have the light that gives life." The Pharisees told him: "You are testifying on your behalf; your testimony is worth nothing." Jesus answered: "Although I am testifying on my behalf, my testimony is valid, because I know whence I came and where I am going. You, you know neither whence I came nor where I am going. You judge according to the flesh, I judge no one. And should it happen that I judge, my judgment is valid because I am not alone, but the Father who sent me is with me. It is written in your Scriptures that the testimony of two people is reliable. So, there is myself testifying on my own behalf, and there is the Father who sent me and who also testifies on my behalf." Then they said to him: "Where is your Father?" Jesus answered: "You have knowledge neither of me nor of my Father; if you had knowledge of me, you would know my Father also."

Jesus said all of this in the Treasury as he was teaching in the Temple. No one arrested him because his hour had not yet come.

Then he continued: "I am going away; you will search for me and you will die with your sins upon you." And the Jews were wondering: "Will he kill himself since he says: "The place where I am going to, you cannot come!" Jesus went on: "You belong to the earth, I come from above; you are of the world; I am not of this world. That is why I told you that you will die with your sins upon you." "Then, who are you?" they asked. Jesus gave this answer: "First of all, I am what I

The Aspects of the Messiah

told you. I have a lot to tell you about yourselves, I have a lot to judge, but He who sent me is Truth itself. And what I have heard from Him, I am proclaiming it to the world." But they did not understand that he was talking to them of the Father. So he added: "When you will have extolled the Son of Man, you will then recognize what I am, you will recognize that I do nothing on my own, and that I am speaking according to the teachings of the Father. He who sent me is with me; He has not left me alone, because I always do what pleases him." While he was speaking in that manner, many believed in him.

Then Jesus said to the Jews who had believed in him: "If you continue in my word, you are truly my disciples; and you will know the truth, and the truth will make you free." They answered him: "We are descendants of Abraham and have never been slaves to anyone. What do you mean by saying, 'You will be made free'?" Jesus answered them: "Very truly, I tell you, everyone who commits sin is a slave to sin. The slave does not have a permanent place in the household; the son has a place there forever. So if the Son makes you free, you will be free indeed. I know that you are descendants of Abraham; yet you look for an opportunity to kill me, because there is no place in you for my word. I declare what I have seen in the Father's presence; as for you, you should do what you have heard from the Father."

They answered him: "Abraham is our father." Jesus said to them: "If you were Abraham's children, you would be doing what Abraham did, but now you are trying to kill me, a man who has told you the truth that I heard from God. This is not what Abraham did. You are indeed doing what your father does." They said to him: "We are not illegitimate children; we have one father, God himself." Jesus said to them: "If God were your Father, you would love me, for I came from God and now I am here. I did not come on my own, but he sent me. Why do you not understand what I say? It is because you cannot accept my word. You are from your father the devil, and you choose to do your father's desires. He was a murderer from the beginning and does not stand in the truth, because there is no truth in him. When he lies, he speaks according to his own nature, for he is a liar and the father of lies. But because I tell the truth, you do not believe me. Which of you convicts me of sin? If I tell the truth, why do you not believe me? Whoever is from God hears the words of God. The reason you do not hear them is that you are not from God."

The Jews answered him: "Are we not right in saying that you are a Samaritan and have a demon?" Jesus answered: "I do not have a demon; but I honor my Father, and you dishonor me. Yet I do not seek my own glory; there is one who seeks it and he is the judge. Very truly, I tell you, whoever keeps my word will never see death." The Jews said to him: "Now we know that you have a demon. Abraham died, and so did the prophets; yet you say, 'Whoever keeps my word will never taste death.' Are you greater than our father Abraham, who died? The prophets also died. Who do you claim to be?" Jesus answered: "If I glorify myself, my glory is nothing. It is my Father who glorifies me, he of whom you say, 'He is our God,' though you do not know him. But I know him; if I would say that I do not know him, I would be a liar like you. But I do know him and I keep his word. Your ancestor Abraham rejoiced that he would see my day; he saw it and was glad." Then the Jews said to him: "You are not yet fifty years old, and have you seen Abraham?" Jesus said to them: "Very truly, I tell you, before Abraham was, I am." So they picked up stones to throw at him, but Jesus hid himself and went out of the temple.

He returned to the Temple at dawn. The multitude came to him; he sat and began to teach.

Later the Scribes and Pharisees brought him a woman caught in adultery; after placing her among the people, they said to Jesus: "Master, this woman was caught in the act of adultery. According to the Law, Moses told us to stone these sorts of persons; and you, what have you to say?" They were saying this to put him to the test so as to be able to accuse him. But Jesus bent down to write upon the ground with a finger. As they continued interrogating him, he stood up and said: "Let him who is without sin throw the first stone." And bending down again, he continued writing upon the earth. When they heard his words, they went out one after another, the elder going first; so Jesus remained alone with the woman who stood there.

Jesus then stood up, and seeing no one but the woman told her: "Woman, where are your accusers? Has any one condemned you?" To which she answered: "No

THE CROWNING OF HIS WORK

one, Lord." Jesus then told her: "Neither do I; I do not condemn you; go and sin no more."

As Jesus was walking by, he saw a man blind from birth. His disciples asked him: "Master, who sinned, was it he or his parents, for him to have been born blind?" Jesus replied: "It is neither he nor his parents who have sinned, but only so that the works of God could be made manifest in him. It is mentioned that I accomplish the works of He who sent me while it is daylight. The night is coming when no one can work anymore. As long as I am in the world, I am the light of the world." Having spoken these words, he spat on the ground and making mud with his saliva, he put this mud upon the man's eyes. Then he told him: "Go and wash this mud in the pool of Siloam" (a word that signifies: the envoy). The blind man went to bathe and returned seeing quite distinctly. The neighbors and people who had observed that he was asking for alms, wondered: "Is this not the man who was seated and was begging?" "Yes, it is he," answered a few. "No," others affirmed, "but he resembles him." Meanwhile, he kept saying: "Yes, it is I." "The people kept on asking: "How were your eyes opened for you to see?" He answered: "The one they call Jesus made some mud, placed it on my lids, then told me 'Go to wash at Siloam.' I went there, I washed, and I see." They continued asking: "But he, where did he go?" To which he replied: "I do not know."

The healed blind man was led to the Pharisees. But it was on a sabbath day that Jesus had made the mud which opened his eyes. The Pharisees asked him how

The Aspects of the Messiah

he had regained his sight. He told them: "He put some mud upon my eyes, then I washed, and now I see." Thereupon, a few among the Pharisees said: "This man does not come from God, because he does not observe the sabbath." Others retorted: "How can a sinner perform such miracles?" They were in disagreement; so they again addressed the blind man: "And you, what do you think of him since he gave you sight?" "He is a prophet," he replied.

Not believing that this man had been born blind, and had recovered his sight, the Jews sent for his father and mother, and asked them these questions: "Is this really your son whom you claim to have been blind from birth? How is it that he sees now?" "His parents answered: "We know that he is our son, and that he was born blind; but how it happens that he can see now, we do not know. Neither do we know who gave him his sight. Ask him, he is old enough to speak for himself." His parents gave this answer in fear of the Jews, because these had already decided that were someone to recognize Jesus as the Christ, he would be thrown out of the synagogue. That is the reason the parents had said: "He is old enough to answer for himself, ask him." The Pharisees called the man who had been born blind for the second time and told him: "Glorify God; we know this man to be a sinner." So he replied in turn: "I know not if this man is a sinner, but I know one thing—I was blind and now I see!" They again asked: "What did he do to you? How did he open your eyes?" He responded: "I have already told you and you were not listening to me. Why do you

THE CROWNING OF HIS WORK

want to hear it anew? Do you too want to become his disciples?" Therefore they heaped insults upon him, saying: "You are the one who is his disciple; we are the disciples of Moses; we know that God spoke to Moses; as far as this man is concerned, we do not know whence he comes." The healed man responded: "That is rather strange, you do not even know whence he came, and yet he opened my eyes! We know that God does not heed sinners; if on the contrary, someone fears God and does his will, that is the man that God heeds. No one has ever heard of anyone opening the eyes of a man born blind. If this man had not come from God, he could do nothing." They replied: "You were born in sin from head to toes and you dare to teach us a lesson!" Thereupon they threw him out.

Jesus, upon learning that the man had been thrown out, and having met him, asked: "Do you believe in the Son of Man?" He answered: "Who is he, Lord, that I might believe in him?" Jesus then said: "You saw him; it is he who is speaking to you." "I believe, Lord," said the man, prostrating himself at his feet. Jesus continued: "I came to this world for a judgment; so that the blind may see and those who see may become blind." Some Pharisees who were present heard those words and asked: "Are we blind also?" Jesus answered: "Were you blind, you would not be guilty; but as you say 'we see,' so your guilt remains whole. Verily, I say unto you that he who does not enter through the door into the sheepfold but climbs into it through another entry is a thief and a brigand. The one who enters through the door is the shepherd of the flock. The

The Aspects of the Messiah

doorkeeper opens the door for this man, and the sheep hear his voice. He calls the sheep that belong to him by name and takes them out; he walks ahead of them and they follow him because they know his voice. They will not follow a stranger; on the contrary, they will flee from him, because they do not know strangers' voices."

Such is the parable Jesus was telling them; but they did not understand what he was referring to, so Jesus went on: "Verily, I am telling you, I am the door of the sheep. All those who preceded me were thieves or bandits, and the sheep did not listen to them. I am the door; anyone who enters through me shall be saved, he will come and go at will and find his fodder in the pasture. The thief comes only to steal, to slaughter, and destroy. I came so that my sheep may have life abundantly. I am the good shepherd. The good shepherd lays down his life for his sheep. As to the hireling, the one who is not the shepherd and to whom the sheep do not belong, upon seeing the wolf arriving, he abandons the flock and takes flight; so the wolf harasses and disperses them. That is the way he acts, because he is but a hireling who has no concern over the sheep.

"I am the good shepherd; I know my sheep, and my sheep know me, just as the Father knows me and I know the Father; and I give my life for my sheep. I have other sheep that do not belong to this sheepfold. These I have to bring in also. They shall hear my voice, and there will be but one flock, one shepherd. This is why the Father loves me; He loves me because I lay down my life to take it up again. No one takes it away

THE CROWNING OF HIS WORK

from me; I give it of my own accord; I have the power to give it; I have the power of taking it back again; such is the order I received from my Father." These words carried consternation and division among the Jews, the majority of whom said: "He is possessed, a madman; why do you listen to him?" Others claimed: "These are not the works of a possessed man; could a demon restore a blind man's sight?"

It was winter and the feast of Dedication was being celebrated. Jesus was strolling under Solomon's portico, in the Temple. The Jews surrounded him in a circle and said: "How long will you hold us in suspense? If you are the Christ tell us frankly." Jesus answered: "I have told you and you do not believe. The work I am performing in my Father's name bears my testimony, but you do not believe because you are not among my flock. My sheep hear my voice; I know them and they follow me. I give them everlasting life; they shall never perish and no one shall ravish them out of my hands. My Father who entrusted them to me is greater than the whole and nothing can ravish anything which is in the hand of the Father. The Father and I are one."

The Jews again brought stones with which to stone him. Jesus told them: "Through the Father I have performed excellent works before you; for which one do you want to stone me?" The Jews replied: "It is not for any deed nor excellent work that we stone you, but because of your blasphemy, because you are but a man, you pretend to be God." Jesus answered: "Is it not written in your Law: 'I said: "you are gods"'? So, your Law has called gods those to whom the Word of God

The Aspects of the Messiah

was addressed (and the Scriptures are incontestable), while I, whom the Father has sanctified and has sent into the world, you accuse of blasphemy because I say: 'I am the Son of God'! If I do not fulfill God's works, then do not believe me. But if I do them, although you might not have faith in my words, at least trust my works; let my actions tell you and permit you to recognize that the Father is in me and that I am in the Father."

Once again, they attempted to seize him; but he escaped from them and returned to the other shore of the Jordan, to the place where John the Baptist had first baptized. He remained there, as multitudes flocked to him, saying: "John, it is true, did not perform any miracles; but everything he told us about this man is true." Thereupon, a great number believed in him.[1]

---

[1] Matt. 20:17–19; Mark 10:32–34; Luke 18:31–34; Matt. 20:20–28; Mark 10:35–45; Luke 22:24–30; Matt. 20:29–34; Mark 10:46–52; Luke 18:35–43; John 7:1–24, John 7:25–52, John 8:12–59, John 7:53, John 8:11, 9, John 10:1–19, John 10:22–42.

Christic Energy

WHEN THE MOTHER OF JAMES AND JOHN ASKS FOR two places of honor in heaven for her two sons, the other disciples are scandalized at this effrontery. Hence, Jesus gives each of them the same lesson with paternal gentility. The kingdom of God can in fact be attained; but the energy of the contender must be aimed in the opposite direction to that of his natural tendencies. The absolute and the relative are opposite modes; no one can follow them both at the same time—one must choose. When working for oneself, one works for the devil; when working for our brothers, one works for God. Everyone does not have the courage to give his life for others as Jesus did; but one can give it in bits and pieces—one might say, in fragmented morsels.

If you want to be welcomed some day by the Father and experience the ineffable joy, the clear sprightliness of his smile, humble yourself, let people take advantage of you, let people grab and discard you, as a child does with the fruit that quenches his thirst; let them scorn, mock, your simplicity disdainfully, let them wound your balsamic hands. Let it happen! Has not the Son of Man said: Be the servants, adding: be the slaves?

Evidently, such conduct will alienate those among your friends who love you through the tenuous threads of matter, of life ether, and of natural mutual affinities. Jesus too was rejected by his family. His disciples, for the most part, also suffered this same exile. Family ties are woven out of the threads of flesh, of possessiveness, common interests. The child whose spirit comes from above is often a stranger among his kin. The brothers of Jesus were ordinary men. In

The Aspects of the Messiah

Jesus, on the other hand, there was nothing terrestrial. His physical body was composed of the purest, the most subtle essence found within all varieties of creaturely mixtures. Between him and other men there could never be any spontaneous sympathetic chords other than the luminous intuitions from the heart; and in fact it is because only what is most noble flows from the heart that his fervent disciples can love and follow him.

He is the veritable "super-man" because nothing that concerns man remains foreign to him. The Jews, by being amazed at his thorough knowledge of the Scriptures, prove they had not understood him. He had a perfect knowledge of the Scriptures, because, might we say, he had dictated them, for he is the ante-secular author of the Book of Life and the Book of Laws. He also knew the Scriptures as a man, because it was enough for him to evoke their spirit through power and upon the very limpid mirror of his own spirit. Always remember that he is the Master; for him there are no fences, no veil, no crypts, no abysses, no inaccessible summits, no jailors, no spies. Everything is present before him; any being, from the infinitely small to the infinitely large, appears to him in its intrinsic nudity.

No one will find this method of knowledge or this mode of teaching, as no one can accept the one and practice the other, unless he first seeks the total fulfillment of God's will. Any other goal, no matter how noble according to human ideals, prevents comprehending the truths contained in the gospels. In any event, the good found in the doctrine brings out the sincerity of the apostle. It is quite probable that those who speak from themselves and who think according to their own authority do not teach the truth. Where these delicate matters are concerned, one

THE CROWNING OF HIS WORK

must challenge and distrust appearances. The laws of nature and of men have no hold at all upon anyone who remains in this superessential internal simplicity. It is understood that, before attaining that state, man has had to endure all slaveries and has undergone all experiences.

So, Jesus comes to the temple, preaches therein, and continues to heal in spite of the wrath increasingly unleashed against him. The human will, in fact, is not all-powerful! Not wanting to make allusions here to the metaphysical entities of ancient Pythagoreanism, let us recall that any event is but the realization of a nexus upon the trajectory of which our karma or providence places us. Theoretically, we can either harbor or drive away this event, but, owing to our weakness of will, we may in reality succeed in advancing or postponing the realization of this nexus. Therefore, the nexus of the Passion could not be modified: neither through the hatred of the Jews nor through the fervor of the disciples; neither in its form, nor as to the timing of its occurrence. Jesus alone, burning from the desire of fulfilling his work, had the necessary power to command the figurative spirit of the Passion, as well as over all beings, because he alone could write upon the Book of Life.

One can discern the motives that impelled him during the last weeks of his life to summon so forcefully the particular characteristics of his work that wounded sacerdotal pride the most: his veracity, his divine filiation, his superiority over the prophets, his independence from traditional rites.

The Civilizing Jesus

WHAT MEN POSSESS SEEMS TO THEM TO BE OF LITTLE value; that which they do not possess seems precious to them. Thus, many who looked at Jesus with indifference when he lived among them, ran looking for him as soon as he disappeared. Some even called for him at all the crossroads of births and deaths from the four corners of the earth. They clamored for him from the summits of the worlds; but, as the magi-king predicts (Prov. 1:28): "They ignored him at times of joy; they will not find him in times of distress." That neglect and this pursuit occur upon the roads of the earth as well as upon those of the soul. However, at certain times the barriers are left open and passage is gratuitous; at other times, there is a toll; occasionally, one cannot pass at all. One must await the following day for the star of the dead to have risen anew.

Are these mere symbols? No, they are realities. The universe is a vast tapestry of symbols only for the philosopher who looks but through the glass pane of his personal mentality; the peasant who goes out into the clear sunlight and looks with his eyes, sees reality. If symbolism satisfies you, remain upon the plane of symbols. But if your humble heart thirsts and hungers for verity, go beyond the philosophical vales, climb the high plateaus of the invisible; advance towards the solitudes, towards the summits that human industry cannot reach; see how everything there is alive, free, simple, real, pacifying, and satisfying.

Then you will comprehend why the last manifestations of Jesus took place in the Temple on the last day of the Tabernacles' Feast, which was on the 22nd day of the seventh month; why he chose this feast, to commemorate the journey through the desert, he, the reality of whom Moses was the token, as the shadow precedes the traveler walking towards the setting sun.

While awaiting the Word, no matter how magnificent had been the civilizations of Atlantis, of Thebes, of Ayodhya, and of Ninevah, men were in the desert. When the Word arrives, they find themselves (if they want to) in the Promised Land. No one, not having had a glimpse of them, can imagine what the eternal riches are; no treasure, no beatitude, no energy from this immense creation could pay for one ounce of it. Rational wisdom is far below the secret wisdom of men, though this latter is but the shadow of the hidden Wisdom of God. If you have not tasted the beatifying savor of the latter, you will not be able to face how it overshoots in one fulgurant thrust of a wing, how it surpasses in one immense unfurling, how it erases with its supernatural brilliance, the limits, the effects, and the lustre of the mysterious wisdom of the Ancients.

Because nothing can pay, Divine Wisdom is free, inexhaustible, total, and definitive. Jesus is the bearer of the amphora. For that which existed before the centuries alongside the Eternal One is a water, since it fertilizes all deserts, starting with that of the original void. Sapience and sapidity are from the same linguistic root. Our heart is a rock; only the wand from the divine Moses could cause a spring of living water to gush forth from it; and because the living water came from heaven, each of its drops contains all the virtue from the inexhaustible infinite.

If for a mere fraction of a second your face could be touched by the breath of Jesus's wings, even if you were the master of the earth, even if you were the god of the Milky Way, you would catch a glimpse of the Spirit, air saturated

The Aspects of the Messiah

with pure energy, water that swells the heart with the ineffable. Through the planetary circles, through orbs, flying comets, and cosmic hurricanes you would be able to perceive the prodigious descent of the Son sweeping the Spirit along in his wake; you would see his sovereign ascension to the Father in the flamboyant eddies of the Consoler, while the suns and stars were receding as nothing more than unknown reddish dots upon the limitless azure of the superior abysses.

The Rear-Guard

ACCORDING TO THE MOSAIC CONCEPTION, A PROPHET is a man who relays to others the words that God has said to him. Now, Christ did not seem to fulfill the conditions of the prophesied Messiah; it was not known that Joseph and Mary were of the race of David. And if the common people, such as the peasants and soldiers, vaguely felt the grandeur of his words, the scholars and powerful did not understand them.

At present, when intellectualism shines more than it has ever done within any of the races that the Deluges have obliterated from history; when poets, philosophers, and seekers seem bound to knock their heads against the vault of the "possible," where subtlety is the uncontested queen, there are no true disciples of Jesus. Those who know that they know, those who are conscious of their genius, those who realize they carry a scepter or a torch, all those (and they are thriving today) who occasionally gather in public centers and churches, who use elegant expressions, who discuss and sustain "theses," arrive in this way at the same conclusion as did the Pharisees, who told Nicodemus: "Get

THE CROWNING OF HIS WORK

informed, study, and you will see that nothing real, beautiful, and good can come out of Galilee, from a nonintellectual center!" And, as it happened two thousand years ago in the shadow of the majestic porticoes of the gold-plated roof of the great Temple, "each man returned home" in the same state of mind. The world changes but little.

As for Jesus, he visits Lazarus, calls on Nicodemus, and goes among the publicans indifferently. Honorable, well-behaved people as well as the riff-raff are equal before his solicitude when they act as the children of Abraham should, meaning: as soon as they indicate wanting to believe in him. Is he not here to save the lost ones, to rehabilitate socially those whom society rejects, to rehabilitate morally those who feel rejected within their own conscience?

How does he save those despairing souls? By impelling them to bolster their efforts. Therefore, the greatest sin is the denigration of life. Beware of those who elevate immobility upon a throne. Inertia is not alive, and what is not alive is precipitated unavoidably to the bottom of nothingness. Let us act by taking action, cost what it may, even were we to stray. Were we living in error, we would still be afloat in life. In spite of itself, error contains the immortal seed of truth within. Let us not seek repose; let us not remain supine when Jesus comes to us. There is always something to be done. There is no more unbearable pain than the one of the outer darkness—this black, ungraspable, amorphous obscurity that surrounds the world, this ocean beyond space, this century beyond time, this place where nothing exists, where the being is lost and dissolves infinitesimally down to its complete annihilation. Extraordinary men have longed for centuries for the immovable impassivity where the poles of the universe stand; their punishment was to finally reach the object of their tenacious efforts; their punishment is so terrible that heaven always lifts and rescinds it long before the laws of ontological equilibrium would have permitted, were justice alone directing creation, and if mercy did not intervene.

Such states of existence are too remote for us to imagine the horror they contain. Just try to remain immobile for five minutes without desires, memories, or thought; yet, your lungs would still be functioning and your vegetative nervous system would continue working. Were you able to reach such total vacuity, you would come out of it suffering unbearable pains in your head and epigastrium. This example may furnish you an idea of what the cult of metaphysical immobility consists of.

Do not think that this picture is grossly exaggerated. Everything in nature is real. The theory of the philosopher, of the aesthete, of the analyst, is but the subjective shadow of an objective being. Awareness, a desire, an act, is but getting acquainted with or making contact with living, real, individual phenomena, which we force to go to and fro, to struggle, suffer, and die. We will experience this later when our nerves have become steadier, more solid, and our will more constant.

What Jesus Is

THE WORD IS LIFE, INTELLIGENCE, CONSCIOUSNESS, the ruler, the principle, the regent, and the goal of all beings. Were we clear-headed, with limpid inner sight, we would see that all of this is the light of lights: Jesus is nothing but the incarnation of the love of the Father (the love of the Father made incarnate); by following him, we eventually reach the Father. And those who disown or deny him are still irresistibly drawn to him.

The Man-God, Christ Jesus knows everything. He is the only being who knows himself totally; otherwise, he would not be the Son of God. Hence, he alone can state whence he comes and whither he goes. He knows what a judgment is, which is why he does not judge. We… we do not know what a judgment is; therefore, fifty times a day we judge people and things. Jesus possesses such profound omniscience that it is immediate, and a power so perfect that it is immobile; his very presence spells out and simultaneously carries out the judgment.

This unity that bursts irresistibly from him spreads over all who accept him. Thus, where a child of God is, there is God; there, where a friend of the Son is, there is the Son, and consequently the Father: the super-essential identity, the incomprehensible harmony, the beatific union.

Thus, the world is dual. One army struggles towards the top and towards the center—towards oneness; the other struggles towards the bottom, towards the circumference—towards the multiple. No one can stand between them. One must walk either with the first or with the second. There are temporary deserters from one banner to the other; but education can only be gotten according to one's capacities—it takes time. When intelligence is limited, it is through the heart that light enters. When our heart is perverted, it is by refining the intellect that we are made to advance. This explains why the Spirit descended here-below only after Christ, who had been his precursor. In proportion as Jesus withdraws from his Father, so the Spirit spreads from one to the other as the most secret, most subtle, most faithful messenger. And, faithful to his nature, he

The Aspects of the Messiah

propagates himself with an irresistible and victorious fecundity here, there, and wherever one of his breaths has been felt.

Therefore, even when he goes down to the bottom pit of hell, Jesus is never alone; the atmosphere of heaven with its inhabitants surrounds him. Men are never alone either. No matter where they are, the spirits who brought them at their birth always remain close by—but it is they themselves who evoked them through their past existences. This is why regeneration is such an immense work, carried out progressively through the intellectually animic and sensible knowledge of truth. And it is truth that in the end, with one stroke, gives man his freedom by giving him life a second time.

In fact, verity (truth) is a live substance. Intellectually, it consists in seeing things as they are, outside of any personal equation or refraction of the milieu. Hence, the seeker must work upon himself and upon that milieu. First upon himself via equilibrium, harmony, and purity; then upon the milieu, by infusing it through his actions and his own serenity. Any notion results in an action. Hence the notion of verity assists us to act well, spares us the recommencements, and in the end will liberates us from the chain of causes to effects—which means to say, liberates us from the world.

Mystically, verity is a "person," a being; and the gospel is but the résumé, the kernel, of the proper means of uniting us to it.

Reason does not understand any of this—not the philosophers' reason only, but even that of the esotericists. Jesus explains clearly, in detail, how much man enchains himself to the god he serves, and how, little by little, he becomes its insolvent debtor. If a richer god pays our creditor, we gain nothing by this change. For us to be liberated, it would be necessary that the one who pays could never claim any dues from us. But as no creature is capable of that, solely the one being placed beyond creaturely natural relationships could do so, for such a being alone is sheltered from change and from need. Such a being is God, or the direct Child of God.

So do the material and immaterial also function upon parallel lines. Our spirits have parents; so do our wills and our bodies. As there is a physiological disposition, a function of our atavism, so are our temperament and character functions of our invisible genitors.

At the limit, which means in the core of our being, we have but two fathers: God or the devil. We express them by exteriorizing them subsequently in an inevitable fashion through our thoughts, our sentiments, and our acts.

The devil is the cancer of creation, the great obstacle, the great enemy. The first thing to which he is the adversary, is life: that is why Christ calls him a "murderer from the beginning." Later, he opposes the image of life and combats truth: that is why he is the "father of lies." Such was the case from the first fresh dawns of the innocent and ignorant world.

Man, on the other hand, has the terrible prerogative of having truth in him; hence, he cannot create a lie, and is twice as guilty when he attempts to. His castigation consists in his inability to recognize truth any more. This is why only he speaks the truth who has never lied to his brothers, or to himself, or to external events, or to his inner convictions. Given that Christ has endured all imaginable temptations and never succumbed, it is easy to conclude that he alone is totally veracious.

The Aspects of the Messiah

After having asserted himself as the Father's envoy, Jesus demonstrates to the Jews that his word is truth, since he who adheres to truth overcomes death and reaches eternal life. Going one step further, he affirms that he knows the One from whom he derives his wisdom and his force. Also, he affirms having known Abraham, and ends with these explicit words: "Before Abraham was, I am." The auditors were thus brought from the notion of a prophet to that of a supereminent prophet, or to the concept of an entity as old as the world. In fact, the Word Jesus is the firstborn among all creatures and the supreme jewel of their universal effort.

Teratology

THIS IS THE SETTING WHERE THE BELOVED DISCIPLE places the miracle of the man born blind, which those who hold the view of reincarnation often propose as proof of their thinking. I myself hold these beliefs as true, but I do *not* believe that knowing about them is indispensable to our salvation. In fact, if we adhere to gospel morality in its essence, it becomes useless and even embarrassing to foresee multiple lives. Although this fact is a proof and sign of the mercy of God, it can also discourage us or mitigate our ardor. Rare are those whose ardor rises to envisage the perspective of a long series of ever-renewed tests and struggles with glee. The great majority aspires to little more than a more or less aesthetic, restful paradise; and if the ordinary man knows that his soul has a series of centuries to amend itself, are there not many chances for his zeal to slacken and for these little recreations known as sin to increase and recur? How true it is that any knowledge bears the burden of responsibility!

THE CROWNING OF HIS WORK

The healing of this particular blind man conceals something other than what modern spiritualists thought they had found out. The lesson it teaches is not symbolic, although the Church tried to suggest this when in the first centuries it chose to have this passage read on the Wednesday of the fourth week of Lent—the day consecrated to the baptism of catechumens. There are all sorts of creatures in the universe.

Here on earth we speak, see, and taste; but on certain other spheres one is mute, or blind, or lacking rational faculties; and elsewhere the non-self is perceived by many more than five senses.

This innocent blind man came from another sphere. Every day we come across creatures in human form who are here for the first time. When esotericism teaches that everything in the world is related, these universal relations do not merely exist on account of vibrations from cosmic ethers. Rather, if all centers receive news from one another, it is especially due to the messengers. Creatures must evolve by passing through a great many ontological states, if not through all of them. Only thus are they able to learn how to accommodate themselves to these diverse environments.

Christ never accounted for the multiple reasons underlying his conduct. Neither does a politician dare do so if he wants his projects to succeed. It is for major reasons that Christ cannot do so: as the center and pivot of the world, he must remain infinitely discreet, for into his hands abut not only the hundred wheelworks of a nation, but the milliards of threads of destinies in the total universe.

Not only did he have to bring the world something new; he also had to regenerate what the world already possessed. And it is in this vein and for this goal that he often made

The Aspects of the Messiah

use of tried and true methods. For instance, we know through Pliny (*Natural History*, XXVIII, 7), through Tacitus (*Histories* IV, 8), and through Suetonius (*Vespasian* VII), that saliva and mud were readily used for ophthalmics in the past. Jesus made use of this procedure, into which he incorporated a spark of creative force thanks to which the entire ocular apparatus, which did not exist in this blind person, was instantly developed. Notice particularly that Jesus made use of the soil on the road, he did not seek it elsewhere, because nature always places the remedy in proximity to the disease. The centaury (knapweed) and the borage that grow around your home will cure you far better than those you would buy at the herbalist.

Jesus is therefore both the light of the world and the workman who makes use of the light to work with; we, his disciples, are but the cells of the body of that workman. Whatever we do has value and depth only as long as we accomplish it in him, by him, under his direction, under his order, and by means of his power. This helps us understand this paradoxical sentence: "He came, so that those who do not see may see, and those who see may become blind." (John 9:35–39) On the material plane he leads the blind who believe in him. while the incredulous who have healthy eyes will become totally blind in two or three incarnations. On the moral plane he gives certitude to those humble enough to mistrust their knowledge to the point of feeling totally ignorant. As for those who feel self-satisfied and pretend to possess truth, he lets them wallow in error. To know is to see with the eyes of intelligence. Human science can unfold only from the apparent connections between objects. By dint of looking for these so variable and complex connections, by dint of experiencing their instability and provisional states, disheartenment is born, followed by lassitude and finally inaction, which benumbs and obliterates our faculties.

Hence, the agent of our moral lapses or falls is, basically, pride. Were the Pharisee unintelligent, he would not be guilty of disregarding the light; but if he thinks himself judicious and cultured, he assumes responsibility for his error.

The Sheepfold

ENVISAGED FROM THE POINT OF VIEW OF THIS REINTEgration, creatures appear as if they were divided into two camps: the one of light, the other of darkness. From the ontological point of view they are divided into humans and non-humans; from the angle of their evolution they are classified as wolves and sheep, as devourers and devoured. Chapter ten of John's gospel analyzes this last aspect.

On the other hand, there are all sorts of sheepfolds: each plant, each sun, each race; humans, infrahumans, and suprahumans each have their own. Each shepherd, who is also the gate to his sheepfold (since he alone knows how to open it) represents one aspect of the Good Shepherd.

No one attempts to enter into the enclosure except to take care of the sheep, or to do them harm. This is why the apartments of creation are closed, and why no one is admitted unless he makes himself known to the guardian. Through their psychurgical practices based upon the development of the various organs of the invisible man, the ancient initiations procured for their disciples the means (during their excursions into the invisible) to open the doors to the apartments corresponding to their personal initiation. Baptism was the common key, as were the pass-

The Aspects of the Messiah

words of some secret societies, which, before these became political, were symbols of pneumatological precautions.

One can enter therein duly or unduly, and in this latter case by ruse or violence. To be recognized by the sheep, by the sheep dog, and by the shepherd himself, one must belong to the same farm—which means having lived and worked with them for the same master, and been subjected to the same rules. The robber or murderer makes use of voluntary or ceremonial magic, of tyrannical or crafty force; a man can exploit another unto death; a lower god can feed upon the life of his devoted followers here on earth, in the beyond, or down-below.

Jesus at this time voices a sentence that it might be prudent not to fathom in depth, for how can we unravel (we who are still in the diaper-stage) what were the secret intentions of the great spiritual leaders who heaped rites, laws, and prohibitions upon our ancestors? "All those who came before me were robbers and thieves," said Christ. Did they usurp their thrones, did they reap personal profit from their force, did they knowingly, wittingly, deform the image of God in whose name they claimed to be acting? We do not know. And according to the spirit of the gospel, it is better not to know, since crowns are promised to the oppressed, the weak, and the innocents.

The assembly chosen from among all the flocks forms the great sheepfold of heaven, whose shepherd is Christ. As he is the master of the shepherds, his sheep are free. Since they belong to him only because they obey him of their own free will, and since they obey him only when they fulfill his will, so he feeds them himself from a substance that is his very life: he is the only Shepherd who gives of himself fully without expecting any recompense. None of the other

THE CROWNING OF HIS WORK

leaders in this universe are as totally kind. Even the best among them expect to reap a reward from their work; in short, they are merely mercenaries.

The Good Shepherd knows his sheep because he has suffered for them; and they know him because, ultimately, they each incarnate one of his wills. Likewise, the Son knows the Father because he is the Father's will fulfilled. From the supernatural point of view of unity, the Son himself is this one plane—the form of the Father. He incarnates progressively to build the world; he throws sparks here and there, which are his sheep, and which go through the cosmic hills in search of him. He knows them, since they come from him; and they know him, they hear his voice, since they are consumed in his pursuit.

The life of the Son is an uninterrupted continuity of gifts and of renewals of himself. Henceforth, we too become one with him each time we give totally of ourselves without being compelled. Subsequently, we can sacrifice ourselves boldly without fear of fatigue, emptiness, or death, since the eternal hearth shining within us shines above all the temporal hearths of temporal lives through which we act, from the depths of hells to the highest of paradises.

In any religion, if the believer accomplishes it perfectly, he becomes a real god for various hierarchies of invisible creatures. Jesus can therefore rightly say: "My Father and I, we are one," since he fulfills the essential religion, since he realizes the divine Law, to the point of truly becoming the living Religion and the incarnate Law. Just as is the sheep is a god for the grass on which it grazes, so is the shepherd a god for the flock he leads.

The Aspects of the Messiah

The Shepherd

THERE ARE ALL KINDS OF FLOCKS, ALL KINDS OF BAD shepherds, all kinds of good shepherds. But these latter are scarcer than the former, because men little versed in evaluating matters conformably to the spirit are unable to discern the light except where it is least veiled—that is, in the religious domain. God manifests himself in the domains of the arts, sciences, politics, and social economy; but men, upon becoming civilized, erected walls between themselves and this supreme God, whom they habitually confuse with "the gods." Intelligence and the most exquisite sensitivity are not sufficient to appreciate the spiritual worth of a work of art, of an invention, of a law—for this, the gift of wisdom is required.

Most of the time, shepherds are recognized by men only within the superconscious centers of intellection. Under certain conditions they manifest themselves to the ordinary consciousness of their sheep. On occasion their name spreads by word of mouth among the crowds, but with the notable peculiarity that their celebrity increases and their renown mounts far more when they adhere to the darkness rather than to the light.

It happens that a leader or a monarch may meet one of these extraordinary men. The evil shepherd eagerly grasps this occasion. The good shepherd, however, is well aware that if someone is incapable of conceiving the supernatural light and of realizing it, it is especially that very man whom destiny will seat at the apex of temporal power. In any case, it is far more difficult for a ruler or leader to acquire sanctity than it is for a poor wretch. In our contemporaneous secret history you have seen examples of such peculiarities.

THE CROWNING OF HIS WORK

Rulers of empires have put their trust in the hands of the illuminati of the left, as well as in the hands of the illuminati of the right; and oftentimes their favor has been greater towards the former than towards the latter.

It seems incomprehensible that God would let "error" override truth; and yet this must be, so that man may learn to choose, so that the good in him may pass through the cup of infernal fire. All the elements we need to make the right choice are provided by experience, which alone can teach us. A theoretical survey of beings and of things only gives us indications; but the experiences we go through are not endured without sufferings. It is only after having explored and experienced a certain number of the forms of the false, of error, that the seed of truth can germinate in our spirit. In similar wise is the obscure effort of the roots, buried in the stench of manure teeming with larvae, necessary for the luminous elaboration of a flower.

By what sign do we recognize the good shepherd? Jesus gives us several clues. The envoy of God does not seek the limelight; rather, he remains in the background, speaks little, attacks no one, does not argue, does not defend himself, he never asks anything for himself, does not hasten to display the marvels he possesses, does not seek to captivate the famous, answers only when asked—in sum, his teachings always amount to precepts of active charity, sacrifice, and struggle against one's self.

In brief, the direct envoy of the Father already knows his sheep. They bear a mark on their foreheads, visible only to him, and he certainly will go in search of them wherever they are, since he comes down to earth for that purpose only. It suffices for the sheep to heed his call.

When traveling throughout the world, Christ used to call

The Aspects of the Messiah

men in a loud voice; but many did not "hear" him because he was calling them through the spirit as well as with the mouth. We must therefore facilitate the opening of our spiritual sense of hearing. We must acclimatize our inner being to the celestial atmosphere of the domains of the Lord little by little, first of all by uprooting it from the domains of the prince of this world. The sole apt procedure to this end consists in the persevering realization of the precepts of the gospel. The somnolent energies of our internal being are awakened through this effort. Within the invisible man, both desire and need are creating the necessary organ; and by constantly yearning for God, our spirit ends by really entering into the kingdom and developing therein. By constantly desiring to see and hear angels, we finally succeed in constructing organs sufficiently subtle for such perceptions.

A mirage is possible only when one employs the artificial methods of magianism or of psychism; or when one does not control the self with an iron-handed discipline. Otherwise, tumbling into spiritual debauchery is inevitable.

We see why men are so often mistaken about the quality of their pastors. The crowd welcomes all kinds of hearsay; the well-educated negate whatever exceeds their intellectual horizon. Moreover, both groups act in concert and unite in generalized slander. Consequently, the voice of the people is but rarely the voice of God; and one could almost set as a rule that if a well-known figure is maligned and calumniated, he most surely belongs to the light.

Beyond the natural foolishness of the public, the indiscreet zeal of their disciples is the other foe of the good shepherds. Such disciples are "merely" disciples. What I mean to say is that so far they have merely elaborated some aspirations and realized almost nothing; they are still lacking in modesty, which knowledge of self procures, and in intelligence, which is the fruit of experience. The ancient adage: "The initiated kills the initiator" is usually verifiable, alas! Thus, in the last fifty years,[1] Europe has seen perhaps two or three true shepherds. Their names might be known to you. You might even know that the greatest of them, a Frenchman, was the most vilified; that he proved once more the truth of the gospel proverb "No one is a prophet in his own country," and that the region where he became most renowned was where his teachings were most distorted and least heeded.

Is the work of the ambassadors of light always sterile? No, but it is a long-dated maturity.

God provided the devil with forces equal to his own only to furnish created beings occasions for deploying their energies to the utmost. The devil did not receive wisdom, however, but only cunning. Wisdom entails an element of free will that hell cannot welcome, since in essence wisdom is but the reflection of veritable life. The Father sends his shepherds, not to bring about the sudden conversion of men, but only to sow seeds that will later ripen—for nothing valuable can be wrought unless man collaborates freely of himself. The Father neither coerces nor compels, since he is always able to grant us an extension of time. It is the devil who is in a hurry, which is what condemns him to ultimate defeat.

As for us, let us be wise enough not to step out of the pasture wherein our Shepherd penned us. Let us not heed calls that might reach us from adjoining enclosures. We are totally ignorant of the projects of the Shepherd; but his

---

[1] This work was first published in 1926.

The Aspects of the Messiah

mystical hounds are on watch, faithful to him unto death. They will execute his orders, they will lead us from valleys to hills, they will herd us in, and at night maintain watch over our rest.

Let no enticing fame distract us from our Jesus, so that when we are solicited, we will answer that Jesus is our sole Master, that he knows where his sheep are because it is he who placed them there, and that he alone will come to fetch them.

But beware lest this refusal to run hither and thither turn into inertia. Remain where destiny has placed you pursuant to the indications of circumstances and to the lights of your conscience. *But*, in the sphere wherein you feel you belong, deploy all your energies, fulfill all your duties; and if you find you have nothing to do, set up undertakings and anticipate the needs of those who dare not express them.

CHAPTER II

The Just Judge

S JESUS was teaching in the Temple, the chief priests and elders of the people came to him, asking: "By virtue of whose authority are you doing these things? who gave you this authority?" Jesus answered: "I too shall ask you a question, just one, and, if you can answer me I shall tell you by whose authority I do these things. Whence did John's baptism come, from heaven or from men?" They began reasoning aside among themselves: "If we answer: from heaven, he will tell us: 'Why did you not believe in him?' And if we answer: 'from men,' we shall have to face the crowds because they all look upon John as a prophet." So they answered Jesus: "We do not know." He in turn told them: "Neither shall I tell you by whose authority I do these things."

"What do you think of this: A man had two sons. He told the first: 'My child, go and work in the vineyard today.' The son replied: 'I shall go, Lord,' but he did not go. Going to the other son the father spoke the same words; this one answered: 'I do not want to,' but he relented and went later. Which one fulfilled his father's will?" "The latter," they answered.

Then Jesus added: "Believe me when I tell you that the publicans and harlots are further up the road to the kingdom of God than you. John came to you for the sake of justice, but you did not believe him. The publicans and harlots believed him; and you who saw that did not repent, neither did you come to believe him."

THE CROWNING OF HIS WORK

"Listen to another parable: There was a man, a home-owner who had planted a vineyard. After having built a fence around it, he dug a wine-press and built a tower; he rented it to some vine-dressers, then left on a trip. When vintage-time came, he sent his servants to the vine-dressers to claim the revenues of his vineyard. So the vine-dressers seized these servants; they beat the first, kicked another, and stoned a third. So he sent his son, thinking: they will respect my son. But when they saw the son, they agreed among themselves: "This one is the heir; let us kill him and we shall collect the inheritance!" After having seized him, they threw him out of the vineyard and killed him. Now, what will the owner of the vineyard do to those vine-pressers when he arrives?" They answered: "He will kill those wretches mercilessly, and will lease the vineyard to those vine-dressers who will pay for the fruits at the end of the season."

Jesus told them: "Have you ever read these words in the Scriptures? The stone which the builders rejected is the very stone which became the main cornerstone. This is the Lord's doing, an admirable work in our eyes. This is why I am telling you that the kingdom of God shall be taken away from you and shall be given to a people who will make it yield fruits. He who will fall upon this stone will destroy himself, and he upon whom it falls will be reduced to dust."

Upon hearing these parables, the chiefs of the priests and Pharisees understood that he was referring to them. They wanted to have him arrested, but they

The Just Judge

feared the people, because they considered Jesus to be a prophet.

"The kingdom of God resembles a king who was solemnizing the wedding of his son. As he entered to see those who were at the table, he noticed a man who was not wearing a wedding-garment. He asked him: 'My friend, how did you enter here without wearing a wedding garment?' The man made no reply. So the king told his servants: 'Bind him hand and foot and throw him into the outer darkness; this is where there shall be weeping and gnashing of teeth. Because many are called but few are chosen.'"

Jesus having entered Jericho walked through the city. There lived a rich man called Zachaeus who was the chief toll-gatherer. He wanted to catch sight of Jesus but could not do so because of the crowd and he was of short stature. So he ran ahead and climbed a sycamore tree to see him, as Jesus had to pass by there. Having reached that spot, Jesus lifted his eyes and addressed him: "Zachaeus, come down in a hurry, because I must lodge in your house today." Zachaeus came down hurriedly and welcomed him joyfully. Seeing this, the crowd kept murmuring and saying: "He has entered the house of a sinner and will lodge there!" But Zachaeus standing before the Lord was telling him: "See, Lord, I give half of my goods to the poor, and if I have wronged someone in any way, I reimburse him fourfold." So Jesus told him: "Salvation has entered into this house today because this man is also a son of Abraham. For the Son of Man came to seek and save what was lost."

THE CROWNING OF HIS WORK

The Pharisees having retired, consulted to trap Jesus with his own words; they sent him their envoys and some of Herod's men, who asked him: "Master, we know that you are truthful and that you teach the path to God in all sincerity without favoring anyone in particular. Give us advice: Is it permitted or not to pay tribute to Caesar?" But Jesus, aware of their malice, responded: "Why do you try to test me, hypocrites? Show me the money of the tribute."

They brought him a dinar. He then asked them: "Whose portrait is this; whose inscription does it bear?" They answered: "Caesar's." He then told them: "Render unto Caesar what is Caesar's and to God what is God's." This response surprised them; and leaving him there, they left.

On that same day the Sadducees, who deny resurrection, came to ask him this question: "Master, Moses has said: 'If anyone dies without having children, his brother should marry the widow, which will thus bring forth a posterity for the deceased.' Among us, there were seven brothers. The older married and died without any posterity; he left his wife to his brother. So it went, down to the seventh. Finally, after all of them, the woman died too. Having been the wife of all seven, whose wife will she be at the resurrection?" Jesus answered: "You are in error, because you do not understand the Scriptures nor the might of God. The resurrected ones neither marry nor are given in marriage, but are in heaven as angels. As to the resurrection of the dead, have you not read the word of God that tells you: I am the God of Abraham, the God of Isaac, the

The Just Judge

God of Jacob. God is not the God of the dead, but the God of the living." The multitude who heard that statement was deeply impressed by his teaching.

Having heard that he had silenced the Sadducees, the Pharisees consulted; and one of them, a doctor of the Law, in order to put him to the test, asked Jesus: "Master, what is the greatest commandment according to the Lord?" Jesus told him: "You will love the Lord your God with all your heart, all your soul, all your thoughts, and all your might. This is the first and the greatest commandment. And here is the second, which resembles it: 'You shall love your neighbor as yourself.' From these two commandments the Law and all prophets proceed."

Jesus finding the Pharisees assembled, put the question to them: "What is your opinion of Christ? Whose son is he?" They answered: "David's." "How then," he continued, "can David, filled with the Spirit, call him Lord when he says: 'The Lord told my Lord: Sit upon my right hand until I place your enemies under your feet?' If David calls him Lord, how can he be his son?" No one dared answer a word, and from that day on no one dared question him.

Jesus then addressing the multitude as well as his disciples, said: "It is in the pulpit of Moses that the scribes and Pharisees are seated; abide by what they tell you and do it. But do not imitate their deeds, because they speak, but do not perform. They tie up heavy loads which they heave upon the shoulders of men; but they do not want to stir a fingertip. All of their actions are done so as to be seen by men; in fact, they wear enormous phylacteries and lengthen the fringes of their mantles; they prefer the place of honor at banquets; the front seats in synagogues; on the public squares they expect bows and to be addressed as master by everyone, they who grab the homes of widows while pretending to say prayers at length. As for you, do not let any one call you master, because only One is your Master, and you are all brothers. Also, give no one on earth the name of father, because only one is your Father: the celestial Father. Let no one call you director either, because you have only one director: Christ. The greatest among you shall become your servant. Whoever exalts himself shall be humbled; whoever humbles himself shall be extolled (*et exultavit humiles*).

"Woe to you, hypocritical scribes and Pharisees, for you close the door to the kingdom of heaven before men! You do not enter it and you do not allow those who want to enter to go in.

"Woe to you, hypocritical scribes and Pharisees, for you scour lands and seas to make one sole proselyte; and when he has become your follower, you make him into a son of Gehenna, far worse than you are.

"Woe to you, blind guides, who say: 'If anyone swears by the temple, it means nothing; but if someone swears by the gold of the temple, he is bound.' You senseless blind men! Which is the greater of the two, the gold or the temple that consecrates it? Furthermore: If anyone swears by the altar, it means naught; but if someone swears by the offering which is on the

The Just Judge

altar, he is pledged. Blind men, which is the greater, the offering or the altar upon which this offering is made sacred? Whoever swears upon the altar not only swears by the altar but by anything it represents. Whoever swears by the temple swears both by the temple and by the One whose abode it is. Whoever swears by heaven, swears both by the throne of God and by the One who is seated thereon.

"Woe to you, hypocritical scribes and Pharisees, for you pay the tithe of the mint, dill, or cumin and you leave aside what is most important in the Law: justice, mercy, and honor. You should have done this and not omit that. You blind guides who strain the gnat in the filter and then swallow the camel!

"Woe upon you, hypocritical scribes and Pharisees, for you cleanse the outside of the cup and of the dish while within they are filled with filth and rapines! Blind Pharisees, scour the inside of the cup and of the dish first, that the outside may be cleansed also.

"Woe upon you, hypocritical scribes and Pharisees, for you are as whitened sepulchers! Outwardly they present a handsome aspect, while within they are filled with bones of the dead and all types of putrefaction. So do you outwardly appear to be just to men, while inwardly you are nothing but hypocrisy and iniquity.

"Woe upon you, hypocritical scribes and Pharisees, for you erect tombs for the prophets, you decorate the sepulchers of the just and you say: 'Had we lived at the time of our fathers, we would not have taken part as accomplices to the murder of the prophets!' Therefore you bear witness to your ancestry as sons of your fathers who slaughtered the prophets. Thus, you do fit in the shoes of your fathers! Serpents, broods of vipers, how will you avoid being condemned to Gehenna? That is why God in his wisdom has stated: I shall send them prophets, sages, and doctors: they will kill some and persecute the others. You will kill some, you will crucify some, you will scourge others in the synagogue; you will pursue some from city to city until the blood of the innocent you have shed on earth will fall back upon you, from the blood of Abel-the-just down to the blood of Zacharias, son of Barachias, whom you slew between the sanctuary and the altar! I am telling you, in truth, that this very generation shall be held accountable for it all!

"Jerusalem, Jerusalem, you who kills the prophets and stones those who are sent to you, how often have I wanted to gather your children as a hen gathers her chicks under her wings, and you refused it! Now your hearth is foresakenly yours, deserted. For I declare that you shall not see me again until such time as you state: 'Blessed be he who comes in the name of the Lord.'"

Facing the treasury, Jesus then sat down, observing how the people were making their offering. Several rich people gave a great deal. Then came a poor widow who put two small coins (worth about the quarter of a penny). Jesus saw her and called his disciples over, saying: "Believe me, this poor widow has put a larger amount than all of the others in the treasury. Because they gave what they had to spare, while she, from the

The Just Judge

bottom of her indigence, threw in all she had. She gave her entire subsistence."

As Jesus was leaving the temple, one of his disciples told him: "Master, notice these stones, see these constructions!" Jesus answered: "You are looking at these large edifices? The day is coming when not one stone will remain upon another. Everything will topple over."

Then he went and sat in the Garden of Olives. The disciples approached him, and taking him aside questioned him: "Tell us when these things will occur and what shall be the sign of your crowning and of the end of the world."

Jesus replied: "Watch and see that no one deceives you; because many will come using my name. They will claim: 'Here I am, Christ.' And they will deceive many people. You will hear of wars and of rumors of wars. Beware of being troubled by them, because all this must come to pass; but the end will not yet be near. Nations will rise against nations, kingdoms against kingdoms. There will be famines, earthquakes, frightful phenomena here and there, and great signs in the sky. These shall be the first pains of childbirth. You will be subjected to torments; you will be put to death, you will be hated by all nations in my name. And many will be caught in a snare, they will betray one another, they will hate one another. And many false prophets will rise up and deceive many. And because iniquity keeps multiplying, love among the greater number will cool. Only he who will have persevered to the end will be saved.

THE CROWNING OF HIS WORK

"But before any of this occurs you will be seized and will be persecuted; you will be brought before the tribunals and thrown into prison; you will be scourged in the synagogue; you shall also be brought before kings and governors in my name. It will be the occasion for you to bear witness in my name.

"First, it is essential for the gospel of the kingdom to be preached all over the world, for all nations to know the truth. Only then will the end come.

"Engrave this well into your hearts: when they hand you over, do not prepare your defence, do not worry unnecessarily in advance as to what you will answer. I shall give you the words to say at the moment when you need them; because I shall give you the word and the wisdom which your adversaries shall be unable to resist or contradict. It is not you who will be speaking, but the Holy Spirit.

"Then shall brother hand over his brother to death, and the father his son; children will rise against their parents and have them perish. You too will be betrayed by your parents and your brothers, by your relatives and your friends; and some among you will be put to death. But not one hair from your head will be lost. It is through your patience that you will save your souls.

"When you see armies lay siege to Jerusalem, know that its desolation is near. When you will see the 'abomination of desolation' spoken of by the prophet Daniel set up in the holy place, then let those among you who are in Judea flee to the mountains and those who are in Jerusalem leave it; let not the one who

The Just Judge

might be on the terrace come down to carry anything from the house; let not the one who is in the fields return homeward to pick up his coat, and let not those who are in adjoining lands return home. Woe to the pregnant women and to those who are nursing in those days! Pray that this not happen, neither in winter nor on the sabbath, because there would be still greater tribulations such as has ever been from the beginning of the world to the present time, and will be evermore. And had these days not been abridged, no creature could be saved; but because of the chosen ones, these days shall be shortened. If somebody were to tell you: Here He is! or, Christ is there! do not believe him. Because many false Christs and false prophets will rise up, producing great signs and wonders so as to possibly deceive even the chosen ones. I have now warned you. If someone tells you that he is in the desert, or in a home, do not believe him. Such as lightning springs from the East and flashes to the West—such will be the coming of the Son of Man.

"Immediately following these days of tribulation, the sun will be darkened, the moon will not give light anymore, the stars will fall from heaven, the powers of the heavens will be perturbed. It is then that will appear the sign of the Son of Man in the sky; then will all the tribes on earth strike their breast and they will see upon the clouds in the sky the Son of Man arriving with great power and glory. He will send his angels, who, with the startling blast of the trumpets will gather the chosen ones from the four corners of the horizon, from one extremity of the sky to the other.

THE CROWNING OF HIS WORK

"Let the fig-tree be used as a comparison, when its branches grow supple and its leaves shoot out, you know that summer is close; so, when you will see those things, you will know that the Son of Man is close by, that he is at the gates. Verily I am telling you that this generation will not pass before all this is accomplished. Heaven and earth will pass, but my words will stand.

"As to the hour and day, no one knows, neither the heavenly angels nor the Son; no one, but the Father.

"Be on guard! Watch! because you know not when the time will come! Similarly to a man who is going on a trip: he leaves his house and puts his servants in charge, each with his assigned task, and tells the one at the door to keep watch.

"Keep watch for fear that your hearts may become hardened through excesses, drunkenness, and worldly cares, and that this day may come upon you without warning. It will be like a net that shall fall upon all those who live upon the surface of the earth. Be vigilant and keep on praying ceaselessly that you may find yourselves worthy of escaping what is going to happen and that you will be able to withstand the presence of the Son of Man.

"Be on guard, because you know not when the master of the house will return, whether it be in the evening or at midnight, with the crowing of the rooster, or at the dawn; beware that if he arrives suddenly, he finds you asleep. So, what I am telling you, I tell you all: Be on watch!

The Just Judge

"Then, the kingdom of heaven will be like the ten virgins who, lamp in hand, went forth to meet the bridegroom. Five of them were foolish, five were wise. The five foolish ones had not provided any oil for their lamps; but the wise ones brought oil in vessels, along with the lamps they carried. The bridegroom being late in coming, they all became drowsy and fell asleep. In the middle of the night a cry arose: 'Here is the bridegroom; sally forth to meet him!' Thereupon all the virgins arose and started preparing their lamps. The foolish ones said to the wise ones: 'Our lamps are burning low, share your oil with us.' The wise ones answered: 'There might not be enough for both of us; it is better you should go to those who sell it and buy some.' While they had gone to make the purchase, the bridegroom arrived and the ones who were ready entered the bridal feast with him; and the door was closed. Finally, the other virgins returned, saying: 'Lord, Lord, open up!' But he answered them: 'Verily, I am telling you that I do not know you.' Therefore, be on watch, for you know neither the hour nor the day.

"Thus too is the kingdom of God such as a man who upon leaving for a trip called his servants and entrusted them with his goods. To one he gave five talents; to another, two; to a third only one. Immediately upon receiving the five talents, the one who had received them traded them for a profit and he got five more. Similarly, the one who had received two increased them to two more. But the one who had received but one dug a hole in the ground and buried the money of his master therein; and after a long absence, the master

THE CROWNING OF HIS WORK

returned and asked his servants for a reckoning. The one who had had five came forward bringing five more. 'Lord,' said he, 'you entrusted me with five talents; here are five more I have earned.' The master told him: 'Fine, you good and faithful servant. You have proven yourself faithful in small things; I shall entrust you with greater ones. Come into the joy of your Lord.' The one who had been entrusted with two talents came forward and said: 'Lord, you entrusted me with two talents; here are two more I have earned.' His master told him: 'Fine, you good and faithful servant. You have proven yourself faithful in small things; I shall entrust you with greater ones. Come into the joy of your Lord.' But the one who had received but one talent came forward saying: 'Lord, I knew you to be a hard man who reaps where you have not sown and who gathers from the threshing-floor sheaves which you have not strewn; that is why, full of fear, I decided to bury your talent in the soil. Here it is; you are now again in possession of what belongs to you.' But his master replied: 'Bad servant, lazy man! You know that I harvest there where I have not sown and that I gather from the threshing-floor sheaves I have not strewn. Consequently, you should have invested my money with the bankers, which I would have taken out with interest upon my return. Hence, take away from him the talent and give it to the one who has ten. As to the worthless servant, throw him into the Gehenna without; there, where tears and gnashing of teeth are found.'

"When the Son of Man will come in his glory and all the angels with him, he will sit upon his throne of

The Just Judge

glory. Before him will all nations be assembled; and he will separate the ones from the others, as the shepherd separates the ewes from the he-goats; he will place the ewes on his right, the he-goats on his left. Then the King will tell those who are on his right: 'Come, you the blessed of my Father! Enter into the possession of the kingdom which has been prepared for you since the creation of the world; for when I was hungry you fed me; when I thirsted, you gave me to drink; where I was a stranger, you welcomed me; naked and you clothed me; sick and you visited me; imprisoned and you came to see me.

"The just will then answer: 'Lord, when have we ever seen you hungry and ever fed you? Be thirsty and that we gave you to drink? When did we ever see you a stranger and took you in? Found you naked and clothed you? When have we ever found you sick or in prison and visited you?' Then will the King respond: 'Verily, I am telling you that each time you did this to the least among my brethren, you did it to me.' Then he will say to those on his left hand: 'Go away from me, you accursed ones, into the eternal fire prepared for the devil and his angels. Because, when I was hungry, you did not give me anything to eat; when thirsty, you did not quench my thirst; I was a stranger and you did not welcome me; naked and you did not clothe me; ill and imprisoned and you did not visit me.'

"They too shall answer thus: 'Lord, when did we ever see you hungry, or thirsty; a stranger, or naked, or sick, or in prison and that we did not help you?' But his answer shall be: 'I am telling you verily that each time you have not done any of these things for one of these little ones, it is to me that you have failed to do it. So those shall suffer eternal punishment while the just shall go to eternal life.'"

The Jews addressing him, said: "What miracle will you show us to warrant your acting as you do?" Jesus replied: "Tear down this temple and I shall rebuild it in three days." The Jews pursued: "It took forty-six years to build this temple, and you would rebuild it in three days!" But, the temple he was referring to was his own body; and after he had been resurrected from the dead, his disciples remembered his sentences and began believing both in the Scriptures and in the words spoken by Jesus.

During the paschal feast, while he was in Jerusalem a great number believed in his name because of the miracles he was performing. But he, Jesus, did not trust them because he knew them all and he did not need any kind of testimony to be informed about anyone whatever. He personally knew what each man was within. He could read their hearts.[1]

---

[1] Matt. 21:23–27; Mark 11:27–33; Luke 20:1–8; Matt. 21:28–32; Matt. 21:33–46; Mark 12:1–12; Luke 20:9–19; Matt. 22, 2, 11–14; cf. Luke 14:16–24; Luke 19:1–10; Matt. 21:15–22; Mark 12:13–17; Luke 20:20–26; Matt. 22:23–33; Mark 12:18–27; Luke 20:27–40; Matt. 22:34–40; Mark 12:28–34; Luke 10:25–27; Matt. 22:41–46; Mark 12:35–37; Luke 20:41–44; Matt. 23:1–39; Mark 12:38–40; Luke 11:37–54; Luke 13:34–35; Luke 20:45–47; Mark 12:41–44; Luke 21:1–4; Matt. 24:1–42; Mark 13:1–37; Luke 21:5–36; Matt. 25:1–13; Matt. 25:14–30; Luke 19:11–27; Matt. 25:31–46; John 2:18–25.

The Just Judge

Pharisaism

AFTER THE RESURRECTION OF LAZARUS, CAIAPHAS, THE supreme high-priest, told the Pharisees: "It is best that a man die for the good of the people, rather than let a nation perish." John calls attention that Caiaphas prophesies without being aware that the words which the nature of his role in life make him pronounce have a different meaning from that which he ascribes to them. The prophet is thus quite unaware, and often unworthy; the "abstraction" of the function undermines the one performing it, who, if he is unworthy or incapable, becomes liable for those faults.

The ascetic writers and moralists have described the obstinacy with which a man turns deliberately away from the good, and the hypocrisy with which he piles up all sorts of excuses to justify his actions against the voice of his conscience. The colloquies of Jesus with the Pharisees offer new examples of this delusion. By ensnaring themselves in their own didactical traps, they cause and sustain a division within themselves and generate a similar division around them—indeed, their life can be a continual struggle among these adverse appetites which they foment.

Corporeal perversity is not as grievous as intellectual perversity, because (according to the parable) he who acquiesces and does not act is guilty, whereas he who says no but then, changing his mind, obeys anyway, surpasses the former. Remorse is found therefore to be a salutary medicine; it is the particular divine medicament the Unknown Philosopher[2] refers to as bitter to the tongue and beneficial for the body. Let us be heedful not to refuse it when the

---

[2] Louis-Claude de Saint-Martin, French mystical philosopher (1743-1803). Also known as the Unknown Philosopher.

great Physician presents it to us. In fact, the phenomena of our interior life are no more isolated than are those of our exterior life. Whatever our conscience perceives is nothing but one of the numerous ramifications of an unknowable movement that contacts a whole series of other beings. And for the same phenomenon to recur some other place in the world there has to be a concatenation of biological combinations whose recurrence is unpredictable and beyond the reach of our will. That is why the action which presents itself to the man of pure intentions is for him exactly the duty and work he can best fulfill. It is also why we must never neglect an opportunity. Moreover, it is as well the reason why, with the case at hand, we must never disregard nor let pass us by the occasion of remorse (forerunner of light), which later becomes the generator of remorse and of penance. If the burning love the Father feels for his children causes him to manifest an ever-renewed indulgence towards them, this does not prevent their disobedience from provoking profound perturbations in the equilibrium of the universe, which can precipitate them into inextricable complications that may delay their development, progress, and happiness for centuries.

When the evil wine-pressers beat up the servants of the owner of the vineyard and kill his own son, they but depict thereby the history of the Israelite people and of humanity as a whole. The vine represents the world. From time to time, the Father sends us prophets who attempt to teach us how, through obedience and love, to offer God the fruits of the vital force he has given us. His mercy never wearies, so he ends up sending us his only Son. If through our perverted obstinacy his only Son is obliged to give up his life for us, seven generations will not pass before suicide or cap-

The Just Judge

ital punishment come upon us as a recoil for our having disregarded the light; whereas the light will proceed towards men who are more willing.

If the world is a field upon which all sorts of plants abound, its vegetation is also a struggle and its harvest a symphony. And the final result of its toils makes it possible for each of its inhabitants to become the tabernacle of divinity by means of the construction of the universal temple. The Egyptian priests knew this providential plan and transmitted that tradition to the kabbalists. In fact, Rabbi Solomon and Rabbi Aberbanel teach that the cornerstone is nothing else but the Messiah.

The king who invites guests to the marriage of his son is the Father. His son is our Lord Jesus Christ. His nuptials are the final reintegration of the universe—or the partial reintegrations that bring creatures into a temporary paradise. The servants, are the angels of God. The friends, the ploughmen, and the fishermen are the mystical soldiers. The guests (the Jews) represent that portion of the human race predestined to each of these reintegrations. Their refusal symbolizes our blind spot, our ingratitude, our selfishness, and our assassinations of the missionaries of light. The crossroads and the vagabonds who filled the hall for the feast represent the human groups that had not been destined by providential design for this particular reintegration—the Gentiles, for example. The man without a cloak represents the lazy, the lukewarm, the immobile, who, although he has suffered, did not make use of his sufferings, who did not earn any merits nor any garment of light. He finds no excuses. The outer tenebrae are the purgatories and the caverns of the second death. Within a race of human beings who must leave the earth at a designated time, very few are there only accidentally, or for a particular purpose. The great majority are precisely attending the school suited to their needs. However, they profit very little from this school, as only a very small number prove worthy of the choice.

This report considers the individual point of view as well as the cosmological, and the material as well as the immaterial, because all beings possess intelligence—even stones, even the creations of art and industry. Upon the earth, this intelligence is not perceptible because the spiritual light is dimmed both within and outside of us. But there does exist a place where this light shines in all its splendor, where all veils are discarded, where everyone communicates with one another, where the tenebrous force of nothingness cannot manifest itself. In this sphere, everything speaks, everything feels, everything knows, everything is blessed. Any pure energy generated by beings in the fulfillment of good is transported by angels unto this plane. This is how the heavenly Jerusalem is slowly being built in the course of the flow of humanities and cataclysms. This is where the eternal temple of God is being built. It is there that the stone of the Word, rejected by men's benighted pride, resumes its place to become once more the keystone of the vault of the edifice against which all discordant wills are being smashed.

The Three Binaries

THIS ULTIMATE UNIFYING CONCORD OF THE UNIVERSAL work could not be obtained through any direct intervention similar to the one that, on another plane, the nihilists advocated. A goal can be attained only through methods analogous to its nature. The harmony at the summit and in the center of the world is accessible only to the forms that shine

The Just Judge

within the center and upon the summit of ourselves. This is why Jesus gives this answer to the Herodians: "Render unto Caesar what is Caesar's and unto God what is God's."

Let us imitate nature, which scrupulously classes all its productions according to their source by returning to the temporal and the civil power all that it furnishes us as commodities in our daily living, such as paying our taxes, serving in the military, and rendering public services; and also, by returning to the spiritual all that we receive from it, whatever there is within us that is permanent, essential, and divine—such is the rule.

Francis André, author of a study on Joan of Arc and the Secret Societies of her epoch (*Jeanne d'Arc et les Sociétés secrètes de son temps*), ascertains that the answer of Jesus, as well as the passages in Matthew 25:14, Mark 10:23, and Acts 6 refer to the economic organization of the primitive Christian society, the renovated, revived organization of Moses, Numa, and of Plato. The members of the community sold their goods in order to transform them into currency for their exclusive use, so as to constitute an official treasure neither available nor utilizable by the other communities. The well-known medal of Boyer d'Agen[3] would be one of these badges, and Mammon would thus be understood to be the symbol of usury.

Let us return to our commentary upon morality. After the question relative to the piece of coin, one faces the case of the woman having had seven husbands. To understand the implications of Christ's answer, one must distinguish reintegration from resurrection. Jesus affirms that one lives,

---

[3] The three medals of Christ found by Boyer d'Agen in 1897 depict Christ during his lifetime, and according to numismatists were made in the first century as a sign of recognition among the first Christians.

THE CROWNING OF HIS WORK

but he does not specify (because it is not essential) whether we live again, or are resuscitated on this earth or elsewhere. The departed live, and for the faithful believers this affirmation is sufficient to render the practices and investigations into spiritualism superfluous.

Strictly speaking, resurrections are multiple. Each individual, upon his return to earth, finds the type of body in the exact state to which his previous tasks had brought him. One retains the same gender, except in very rare cases of progress, or of extraordinary regressions.

Let us imagine this same individual arriving close to the end of his cosmic voyage, when the series of his terrestrial and extraterrestrial lives has been concluded. He has experienced all the situations comprised in his destiny; he has arrived at the zenith of his perfecting. From then on, gender, intelligence, physical and psychical faculties, all the turmoils endured by his successive personalities, disappear. He is ready to enter the kingdom of God as soon as he will have received the supreme purification of the baptism of the Holy Spirit. The total number of creatures is infinite; when their work has been fulfilled, they will rest in the Lord. The diverse struggles of existence that were dependent upon the differences of gender are but schools, just as are all the other conditions of relative life. As soon as knowledge of material life upon all levels has been acquired, the life of the spirit begins, where there exists no more struggles, oppositions, or poles. Gender, whether male or female, becomes useless, regardless of what Plato states: souls, the divine foci (nuclei) in the core of each man have no gender.

Thus the Savior establishes, in the ontological as well as in the sociological planes a division between the two domains, the eternal and the temporal. And he demonstrates, when answering a third question, how the disciples must solve this binary by means of the unification of will, intelligence, and power—all three contributing to the fulfillment of the orders from heaven.

We must admit that we cannot execute the first commandment. We can express love of God systematically through our actions; we can meditate upon its flawless beauties through multiple voluntary efforts; but those only can love him who in their hearts possess soul-power; and no man can love God with his whole soul, since no man knows his own soul. That is why the second commandment, which proposes to us to love our neighbor as a school for the love of God, intervenes. Our neighbor is tangible, palpable. We know him, and by analogy we can imagine what his sufferings are. From this, through thinking what our own sufferings would be were the same ordeals to befall us, is born compassion. Then comes unselfish, spontaneous compassion. So, the sum-total of efforts having been accomplished, by accumulating little by little upon the terrain of our spirit, the cells that have been spent for love of our neighbor will form the humus whence the seed of the love of God will draw its sustenance and then grow at a later date.

Love of our neighbor is, if not impossible, extremely difficult. But if through sheer will-power we finally perform the necessary actions, no matter how much antipathy we feel towards that neighbor, love will follow and heaven will show itself satisfied with our courage.

The Whitened Sepulchers

JESUS AGAIN INSISTS UPON THE OBEDIENCE WE MUST observe towards our civil and ecclesiastical superiors: "Do all that they shall tell you to observe, but do not do as they do, for they speak words which they do not fulfill."

In reality, to be invested with any kind of authority is a heavy burden. In the invisible, the first effect of power is to bind the one who exercises it to the strictest observation of the law, the execution of which he supervises.

If someone tells you: "Be charitable, give alms," he is guilty if he is not doing the same because of the bad example he sets, because he prostitutes the word of the law, and because he is also guilty for his personal omission. Happy is he who has but to obey!

Here again the Messiah delivers us because he says: "you are all brothers, you have but one master and but one physician who is Christ, and but one Father who is the heavenly one." Were we really able to believe these words, how many gnawing anxieties would we escape, how many useless efforts, how many complications would be cast away from our hearts and intellects like the superfluous clothing shed by the runners of marathons!

Thus, to decree complicated observances; to take money for prayers recited inattentively, or not even said; to convert by force or ruse; to prevent others from educating themselves by means of prohibitions or cryptography; to alter the real meaning of the laws of heaven via partial commentaries; to seek formulas above acts and feelings; to enjoin hypocritical virtue—these are the seven great sins that the religious leaders of humanity risk committing. Examine them for a moment and you will perceive the disorders, errors, false lights, and illusions whereto they can precipitate the faithful.

Moreover, many things in our civilization are similar: unctuous politeness, memory lacking intelligence, intelligence devoid of morality; eloquence concealing crooked schemes, facades, and, within the home, arguments, debts, and fights; well-educated, hard-hearted and vain children; beautiful but godless school buildings, magnificent temples bereft of saints; beautiful stores filled with junk, manufactured sham-goods; some visual trick and no genuine art; prettiness but no beauty; decorated scientists who profit from the real behind-the-scenes researchers; orators without ideas—these are all large empty platters, and more often than not, repatched, replastered sepulchers.

Let us recall that it is the inner that produces the outer; and let us imagine what a paradise our social state would be if it were disentangled from all hypocrisies.

The light comes from above, from the center; darkness comes from below; though we may cleanse our body, our soul remains sullied; by purifying our soul, our body ends up being healed. How can we purify our soul? By purifying our heart, by overcoming selfishness, and by giving.

Alms-giving is not merely done with cash; everything that belongs to us, everything that constitutes our being, everything we believe to be our property—all of it may be part of the alms. Our money, time, muscles, affections, ideas, discoveries, art: all this may all be given, must be offered, to whoever asks for it, especially to the poor too ashamed to beg, hence to whoever dares not ask.

By doing this, remember that you are not doing anything extraordinary. Alms-giving is part of the general course of nature. No being continues to live unless other beings continue giving to him. That is why selfishness evokes death, while altruism brings life. That is why any being, man, city, or nation, that vampirizes its milieu dies a horrible death. Thus did Oudh, Balk, Thebes, Nineveh, Jerusalem, and

Rome die: for the inhabited world they had become frightful corroding cancers.

Giving is not sufficient, there is a way to give. Were a philanthropist worth twenty million dollars, by giving one of those millions away, he is depriving himself less than does a laborer who gives twenty cents. Also, the philanthropist is recompensed in the worldwide press, which vaunts him, honors him through inscriptions upon marble plaques that will remind future generations of his largesse. Therefore, if you want it to be God himself who recompenses you, see to it that no one but he will learn anything of the gift; and then, try to give not only from your excess, but a little of what seems essential to you.

The Sanctions

JUST AS NO CREATURE IS ISOLATED IN THE WORLD, neither does an event come by itself; everything, things and people, belong to families. No being is born, no event takes place, without its having been foretold. This remark was the point of departure of the grand esoteric science of omens; and Christ confirms it by enumerating the precursive signs of the judgments in his lifetime already inscribed into the book of the future.

We have already seen what one must understand by judgment—that judgments occur ceaselessly all along the course of the universal evolution within all the categories of being. Christ points out the seven precursory signs of the judgments, which are:

1. The manifestation of false adepts, each of whom claims to be the true Messiah. Those who are aware of

The Just Judge

our contemporaneous spiritual movements must have noticed that in recent years the leaders of two sects in the United States, as well as a Hollander, an Algerian Israelite, an Indo-Portuguese half-caste, a Belgian spiritualist, a French magnetist, and a Yogacharya Buddhist, have claimed to be a reincarnation of Christ. On this basis, it is quite probable that this phalanx of so-called saviors will augment rather quickly in years to come.

When the Father manifests himself directly, his terrestrial messenger seeks no publicity, does not advertise, never speaks of his knowledge or of his powers. This is an absolute rule. Hence, do not be affected if a thaumaturgist makes himself known by using propaganda and seducing the crowds. Heaven asks us merely to do our duty. If we fulfill it as best we can, it is enough for our names to be transcribed in The Book; and our Friend will find us very easily, whether in the fields, in our shop, or in a palace. The Lord does not need to advertise himself. Do not chase after hearsay, for uniquely outward manifestations are a path to darkness. Keep away from "gods." Christ will manifest himself in a second, as a flash of lightning, to all humankind, by which time his word will have resounded in all corners of the world.

2. The multiplication of secret doctrines always brings a recurrence of secret societies. Since the earth has existed, never has an esoteric college failed to go astray, and sooner or later deviate into a secret political society. To this, add the economic malaises due to the development of materialism, from which dissensions

THE CROWNING OF HIS WORK

are born. Then come seditions, and finally, wars. Such is the second sign.

3. Men thus give to earth the example of discord, of disobedience, and of cruelty. Through an automatic mechanism that we have glimpsed previously, this intellectual and social disequilibrium becomes geological: earthquakes follow, the immediate cause of which is owing to the inclination of the earth's axis upon the ecliptic and to disturbances within the subterranean magnetic levels.

4. The soil becomes contaminated and goes on strike. Exhausted from intensive cultivation, its life parched due to the materialism of the cultivator (who does not use the beneficial aids that previously religion had procured for him), famines ensue, fomented by the greedy manoeuvres of the monopolizers.

5. The identical causes trouble the fluidic atmosphere. Life impairs them, following which morbid agents multiply; air does not restore us any more; solar heat and light lose their "microbicidal" virtues, whence originate epidemics.

6. Since everything in nature is interlinked and the earth deviates from its orbit, those revolutions repercuss in that part of the stellar system that belongs to our planet, just as they were transmitted to us through the stars of which we are tributaries. Due to these various causes, the aspect of the firmament changes: the celestial bodies move with vertiginous speed, and it is even possible for one of them to fall upon our globe, as

The Just Judge

certain traditions reported having occurred prior to the last general deluge.

7. During this period, the friends of God will be oppressed, persecuted, and imprisoned, because it will be the epoch of the final and most violent revolt of hell against heaven. Turmoils, persecutions, iniquitous sentences, prison, death (all of which may even come from relatives) are what disciples must expect to undergo, thus enabling the light to be present everywhere, in order that it may proffer itself as fodder to the darkness. These sufferings will be unprecedented, and the chosen ones would never be able to endure them without succor. They will have to bear everything with profound submissiveness, with no movement of violence, no rebellion—thus enabling the angel of mercy to descend and inhabit this earth.

Men do not realize the power of gentleness, of meekness. For instance, during these last few years, had the Church chosen not to defend herself, either with polemics or protestations, or through clever manoeuvres, she would not only have atoned for her ancient wrongdoings but would also have regained in a few years the preponderant place she had in the Councils of Europe two hundred years ago. The priests did not trust heaven; heaven abandoned them to their own devises; and we will soon witness the result of their presumptuousness.[4]

The seven signs we have just enumerated—the first of which is the most visible—correspond to the seven signs foretelling the birth of a new race. A judgment can be indi-

---

[4] This was written in the early twentieth century, before 1920.

THE CROWNING OF HIS WORK

vidual, psychic, vegetable, and mineral, as well as social. In each of its procedures, the amateurs of Hermeticism could rediscover the seven omens aforementioned, as well as through occult research, and, in particular, in the preparation of the stone of the philosophers.

All of this belongs to the regime of Justice.

Then comes the divine intervention of grace. As we have noted previously, each race of human beings builds an invisible temple, of which stone temples are but the materializations. When men have become perverted (as was the Israelite sacerdotal priesthood, for example), they destroy the invisible temple—and they call forth the Titus who will destroy its physical image as well. And the Word, if he so wishes, can rebuild both the essential and the formal temple in three days. All thaumaturgies whose principle is divine are governed by the number three. On that subject I could relate many an anecdote. The natural march of phenomena also goes by threes. A miracle, in short, is but an acceleration of this march. So that evolution, a judgment, and the paradisiacal repose that follows it may perchance be accomplished in a very much shorter time than the actual order demands. Thus, a man who is born minus one of his arms or legs usually needs three incarnations for his body to become normal again; but an Envoy from Heaven can cure his infirmity in three days.

See how right it is to work to acquire full control over oneself through patience. He alone who accepts the test with resignation, who does not fear it, does not panic, running hither and thither to escape it—that one does not waste the energies of his body and heart in vain. A prudent measure, so you think, would be to bypass cities, centers that the torrent of civilization transforms into vampires and

The Just Judge

cancers of the people, where all the refinements of selfishness, all the vortices of cupidity, have their rendezvous. No. Stay where destiny has placed you. You are there because it is the best spot for your soul and for other souls; there, where circumstances have affixed you, is where the threads of the work you are especially fitted to perform intertwine; there, you will find the test exactly portioned out to your strength; there, all the lights you are to assimilate and that are healthy for you converge. Life is so short; it is nothing but just a second's pause in the great cosmic voyage. Why should we worry and be disturbed? The schoolboy cannot choose what he has to learn; it is the master who chooses for him and assigns the lessons for the oncoming year.

We have tirelessly searched for proof of this sentence: "Believe me, this generation will not have passed, before all this is accomplished." The destruction of the temple and the Roman war have served religious writers to interpret this text; but during that period of massacres there had been no remarkable innovators or extraordinary epidemics or universal cataclysms. Had the commentators read the Talmud, they would have learned that the doctrine of successive lives was in vogue among the Jews, and that there were laws that, according to the kabbalistic rabbis, presided over the revolutions of souls. Souls, in fact, arrive upon earth in groups, live as groups, leave and return again as groups. These are the groups Jesus refers to as "generations." The ensemble of those who lived in his time and who heard his foretellings will be back again when they are to be fulfilled—that is what he meant.

It suffices for us who surmise what Jesus is, to know that Jesus, having said these words, will cause this essential army of souls to return to earth for that particular moment which these prophetic words have inscribed upon the white pages of the Book of the Future. For it is certain that the Word is the sole reality, the unique immutability, the only permanence. It is evident that everything passes away, since heaven, the earth, and beings are but the forms and shadows of this very Word.

Do comprehend how ineffective and trivial the sublimest creatures seem when in the presence of the Word. They cannot do anything without him. Strictly speaking, they know nothing outside of what he is willing to tell them! Yet, know serenely and with certainty that no one can, or ever will, be able to tell what the designs of God are—whether Christ will return in America, or Persia, or India; whether he will be here soon or in a thousand years. It has often been repeated how Judgment Day will surprise men as much as the fisherman's net surprises the fish. How small is our trust in God to attempt to find out regardless, and how laughable is our pretentiousness! Let us remain awake; let us be ready. This denotes the supremacy of conscience. We should never lose our self-control. As soon as we experience surprise, fascination, or charm, we feel at a loss, in a state of inferiority—our spirit is not present, and it could happen that we be attacked unexpectedly.

All men are overseers of a small portion of the divine domain. Among them are the "soldiers" who owe their post directly to the Master. They exert a much greater influence and shoulder a heavier responsibility, but their salary is also more precious, since they become the friends and equals of their Master. It is comprehensible that if one of them fails to do his duty, he becomes guilty of subsequent great disorders, which is why Matthew has a profound reason to teach us that he will then be rejected among the hypocrites.

The Just Judge

Within the central invisible light, the "soldier" of Christ is recognizable by the uniform he wears. A multitude of spirits have their eyes focussed upon him, just as on earth the underlings follow the same conduct as their leaders. If an administrative director is delinquent in his functions, all his employees will become negligent. However, when a disorder occurs in the invisible, it is far more difficult to set it aright. On the other hand, sincerity is not a metaphysical abstraction; it is a virtue, an acting force, an organ of our spirit, just as much as the larynx is an organ of our body. Sincerity, similarly to each of our powers, has two forms: the first is the accord of our acts, our gestures, and our words with our conscious feelings; the second is the accord of these feelings with our supernatural interior light, which is the root of the first. By definition, the "soldier" knows that light, and so never errs by ignorance; hence, when he errs or sins, it is through a sort of intimate lie, by hypocrisy.

However, most people obey either because of fear or because of love. The soldier obeys only because of love. We therefore conclude that his disobedience is hypocrisy since he is lying to himself, besides which he is also lying to someone from whose sight it is impossible for him to hide.

To sum up: we must work by day, giving of our best so that at night, during sleep, we may receive ample provisions of forces, ideas, and instructions. Such is the example given us by the Savior.

The Day and the Hour

WE HAVE EXPERIENCED WARS AND REVOLUTIONS. Everywhere kingdoms are fighting kingdoms. Here and there are famines and epidemics. Will we undergo the great earthquakes and see the great prodigies and the great wonders and signs in the air and in the heavens as foretold in the gospels? Will Christians be persecuted everywhere, as they have been these past few years in several places?

Nowhere does the gospel state that those terrible days could be avoided. However, the Father's justice is always ready to be moved, tempered, due to the constancy of an infinitesimal proportion of intrepid servants. Already in the early years of this twentieth century it was sufficient that a dozen among them accept a surplus of tests and ordeals for the dates of the predicted tribulations to have been postponed. Why should we not attempt to obtain the delay of the accounts due, remissions, adjournments, alleviations for the benefit of our brothers—this pitiful horde, who neither want to hear nor to see anything of the tidal wave that might engulf us all—our small merits notwithstanding? While presenting these ultimate catastrophes as inevitable, does not Jesus invite us to implore eternal mercy, since he gives us the means to escape these ordeals and to resist these seductions? Man, face to face with God, man clinging to God, man prostrating himself before God, experiences the urgent need of always attempting the impossible.

I want to take you beyond the known surroundings of personal salvation. Open your eyes upon a new day, breathe in a purer atmosphere. I want to incite you to be concerned about the salvation of your fellowman, not only the salvation of those you love, all those for whom you feel sympathy, but for all those who will turn a deaf ear to your exhortations, those who remain insensible to your examples; in short, the multitude of prodigal children not yet full-sated from illusions and sordid pleasures. These are the ones for whom I would like to see you exert your energies,

The Just Judge

because to work for the indifferent, to waste your energies for the ingrates, to pray for those who will never know you are sacrificing something for them and who, were they to learn of it, would refuse to believe it—these are the means that permit you to remain closer to our Master.

I believe you to be capable of living at this spiritual altitude. Try it, and if your faith invites you, together with the help of God, we will weather the mystical passage that the world calls the cape of Tempests, but that we know to be the cape of Good Hope. Jesus offers you several precepts to protect you during these ordeals, to reap all benefits therefrom, for you to help the greatest number of your brothers to endure them successfully.

First of all, from the spiritual angle, to be on guard against those who claim to be Christs or those who announce the return of Christ. No one, as you know, can predict this visible public return, because it is tied in with the Judgment date, and that date the Father will fix by advancing or postponing it without telling anyone, not even his Son. Those false Christs, teaching marvelous things, operating prodigies, will always start by preaching love among humans, peace and unification. After having drawn and attracted the crowds, so tired of strife and false hopes, to themselves, they will prove to them how anyone can become a Christ if he wants to, and they will demonstrate how, in order to attain that aim, one must isolate oneself, withdraw from life, or develop all the energies of the self through self-will—or else, by learning all about the universal mystery by the sole means of exercising one's reasoning power. They will present syntheses that are apparently unimpugnable; they will have command over nature, over the elements, over credulous men. And slowly, without their students becoming aware of it, they will erect the cult of pride and force.

The danger in psychisms, mentalisms, and occultisms resides in the classification these systems bring to our ignorance, and in the satisfactions they seem to procure to our humiliating powerlessness. Whenever you see a miracle, remember that it might have come from the force of darkness. And when confronted by a doctrine that does not accept Christ as the sole Son of God, as God himself, remember that the Adversary is a thousand times more subtle and intelligent than the wisest among men. When you will see Christ, when you will hear him—because we will see him and hear him—from the depths of your very being will come both a certitude and an unimaginable, incomparable peace, which will procure you a conclusive proof. Therefore, beware of stupefying prodigies or seductive theories; know that you must examine your conscience and free will. If need be, when the seduction becomes unbearable, close your eyes, close your ears. When Christ comes to you, he will use the right expression, the true words, and make himself known to you.

During these troubled, bellicose times, Jesus exhorts us to continue practicing charity in our daily lives. In spite of ingratitude from those you succored with beneficence, of scorn from all those whose burden you shoulder, of mocking and hate on the part of those you love—parents, children, husbands and associates—nothing must stop you from continuing to help and cherish them; not even when your generous intentions are misinterpreted, your indulgences ridiculed, your truthfulness incriminated. Nothing must alter your serenity. You will be saved by your invincible patience. Cling to Christ, because the Adversary is ten

The Just Judge

thousand times stronger than the strongest of men, and only Christ can vanquish him.

Christ is the door that opens unto eternal life; his friends are the little doors that open unto Christ. Be vigilant. Keep watch over your body and your heart. Before obeying your slightest impulse, verify whether it conforms to the gospel. Examine your appetites before satisfying them, your words before pronouncing them, your desires before realizing them. Any passion, any fixed idea, any habit is a soporific for our spirit. Keep awake, ask for help ceaselessly—the help indispensable during the storm.

You all know that Jesus is the Son of the Father, you know it only because he revealed himself to you once upon a time, upon this earth. Guard this inestimable pearl carefully from any thieves. When our Christ returns, you will know him at first glance, and you will feel ready through the Spirit to leave this world forever. He will take you towards other fields, other skies, towards a new sun that has been comforting you, unbeknownst to you, for many years. Your future is now made firm; you have nothing to fear. Hence, use all your energies for the benefit of your less clairvoyant brothers; give them everything you have received. You will thus be able to open their hearts to love, and love will enrich you with unknown treasures, regenerate you with inexhaustible forces, finally liberate you for the eternal fulfillment of the beatitude promised to all.

In the turmoil wherein we see almost everyone wallowing, are you not aware that the example of your calm, your certitude, your judicious activities, attract many beings in your wake who in spite of their apparent self-confidence know deeply within themselves that they have lost their way? I do not ask you, or rather heaven does not ask you, to be looking for difficulties, but at least do not shirk those that present themselves; rather, welcome them fearlessly as necessary tasks. The fact that they come to you signifies that you are capable of dealing with them. Within each gesture, each word, in a single glance, heaven may shine through. Do not dim its light—such must be your constant concern. Thus will each of your days shine more attractively and liberatingly for your brothers.

Patience

WHAT A RARE VIRTUE IS PATIENCE, WHICH CHRIST lauded so much when he said: "Possess your souls with patience." No matter how we understand the word *soul*—be it the soul of each auditor, the multiple souls attached to an individual, the *nephesch* or the *ruach*, or even the divine spark in our center—the Christic word is literally exact. To be patient, to suffer, to be resigned and bear hardships serenely, always means paying the debt contracted once upon a time by that part of our being which undergoes suffering—whether it be the body or one of its organs, our double or any of its etheric centers, the spirit or any of its inhabitants, etc. At the end of the test, that suffering part or organ comes out of the darkness. And, as heaven has decided that, although a useless servant, man will receive in fief everything he overcomes from the empire of evil, these fluid ethers, these cells, these subaltern beings, become our property. Bit by bit, patience progressively procures us to possess our souls as our very own. And at the end, this excellent soul, the divine spark, also enters within the enclosure of our spiritual domain.

Chronic illnesses offer us another advantage: they teach

The Just Judge

how very insignificant we are. They give us time to repent. They oblige us, through suffering, to pray. By utilizing them in this fashion we become worthy of being healed and thus capable to recommencing a new life, because humility is an abyss the bottom of which is in the infinite.

No matter how much effort we exerted in doing good, lapses are still frequent. And prayer can always augment our ardor.

⊕

More than ever are the fields of social life becoming battlefields. The Christian must not remain unaware of these strifes, but according to the tactics and strategy of the gospel he can only use spiritual weapons to fight with. Besides weapons, the soldier must possess vigor and the art of wielding them. Our weapons are ourselves: the forces of our body, the passions of our soul, the faculties of the intellect, the powers of the will. Let us learn how to keep them in serviceable condition and utilize them advantageously.

This is an arduous science and a sublime art. I do not pretend teaching them to you. We will simply recapitulate a few familiar views, and together reiterate a few evident maxims, just as the soldier does before going into battle when donning his equipment in precise order and gathering (along with the beloved mementoes of his loved ones) all his hopes and energies.

Today, the laical moralists and liberal Protestants place social action at the forefront of man's duties. But they consider that this must be undertaken independently of the ideas one professes regarding Christ. Moreover, they believe that whatever the ideas behind them may be, philanthropic action remains always whole and good.

THE CROWNING OF HIS WORK

Contemporary Catholicism is closer to the truth when it teaches that any social action must be done for Christ.

All these men, no matter how sincere and serious they are, forget the spiritual factor. Evidently, an action possesses its own value, but this is a material value, whereas the soul of the act, which is to say the sentiment that inspires it, is a true capital value. The spirit of the act, which means the ideal in honor of which it is accomplished, is also a value—the most important of the three. Doubtless, to someone who looks at life, laziness, vice, stubbornness, and obstinacy appear to be the causes (alas!) of the majority of sufferings we would like to alleviate. As one gets older, it becomes more difficult to maintain our illusions regarding the inborn goodness of human nature. Therefore, merely humanistic philanthropy quickly becomes positivistic, rational, and cold. To restore its basic warmth and life, it needs a superhuman motive, a divine motive—it needs Christ.

Thus the education of the will for itself, or the education of the will towards social work, or the education of the will to serve Christ better, are three identical works in their methods, but fundamentally different in spirit.

What is the will? It is the power of amassing and combining all our forces towards realizing what we decide to do. Violence, prejudice, rank obstinacy, are but its excesses or weaknesses. Will denotes having self-control, and means exercising our free will. It is the most important power of our conscious being.

Man is meant to develop himself in order to reach perfection. To what purpose? To become strong? To escape suffering? Or is it to help his brothers by his fulfilling God's plan? This is the true goal—the first two are false.

Which methods should he employ? The artificial devel-

The Just Judge

opments of esotericism along with their Anglo-Saxon surrogates, or the natural procedure the gospel indicates? It is to the latter that my preference goes. Because existence is not merely mental or sentimental, it is especially real and fraught with actions. To be fruitful and full, it doubtless exacts having an intense inner life pursuing ethical, aesthetic, and intellectual unfoldments, along with demanding an outer life just as intensely filled with performing our duties as well as altruistic endeavors. We are earthly; we cannot get rid of matter by negating it; we can only do so by spiritualizing it. The spiritual libertines—Jean-Jacques Rousseau (1712–1778), Pierre Charron (1541–1603), and Jules Simon (1814–1896)—were no more right when they preached a religious system devoid of a temple or ceremonies than are those today who think they can seek perfection solely through meditation, solely through ecstasy, solely through athleticism, esthetics, rites, or by means of respiratory exercises or stimulants.

Man is a small universe. To become perfect, he must call upon all of his means, but without ever letting the means become an end. Man is a cell of humanity; he will develop only by living *with* others, then *for* others.

In short, man takes pains only for love: self-love, love for family, love for humanity, love of God; but only in love of God can he find the strength to overcome the lower attractions of self-love and the often bitter disappointments in family love and philanthropy. May the love of God become our sole motive, our sole aim, and our method.

One cannot live in a constant state of enthusiasm, or create derivatives to increase our enthusiasm. Above sentimental love there has to exist a love of reason—an intellectual, a calm love. When some inner crises occur that prevent our thought from deploying serenely, they can reduce our intelligence, our affective organism, even our nervous organism, to chaos. Then intervenes the will to love, the most spiritual form of love. Whatever the psychic or physical state man may find himself in, however complex may be his business worries or the turbulence of his passions, if he wants to he can always act conformably to love.

To want what God decrees—that is the secret of our perfection. Once we know that, and are intimately and profoundly certain of it, two methods present themselves to the Christian. The first, being prudent, divides up the work and attempts to overcome the diverse weak points of our self-governing by isolating them one at a time. The second, more mystical, more evangelical—but which entails profound humility—demands our total abandonment into Christ's hands. It divests us of self-interest; it prepares us to face all eventualities. Because our concern for perfection limits us, it might even close some spiritual avenues that at the moment are invisible. From the time of this complete sacrifice, Christ takes the disciple along with him, and though respecting the armature of his own destiny, he changes its atmosphere in such a manner that whatever happens to this disciple, it becomes to him a sign of divine will. It is then up to the disciple to carry out this will—in his duties, occupations, pastimes; within his studies, enterprises, sentiments, and opinions; in his relations with others through obedience, orders, or mutual aid; down to his demeanor, his walk, his language, even his clothing.

It has to be done. It must be done with calm and optimism. We must say "Forward" and "Yes, I accept." Just as one does not cure a drunkard by coercion, neither will we overcome our weaknesses or vices by strangling them, but

The Just Judge

rather by creating within ourselves their corresponding virtues. We therefore return to St Augustine's saying: "Love, and then do as you want," since we have chosen the purest love, and since it is the intention that vivifies the action. As an example, here comes the hour we had decided to use to catch up on all the letters that our laziness had put off. But, there is a sick neighbor, bedridden, who needs help. We choose to go to him to bring him solace; this is preferable to having won the little battle over our negligence.

Such is the basic spirit of a Christian education of the will.

You are well aware that other systems exist. Taoism, Buddhism, and the various Yogas are wise and strong schools for the training of the will. It would be presumptuous for me to describe them down to their least nuances, because even very few Orientals are aware of them all. But, in a few words, I would characterize them thus:

> Their dogmas: the existence of numerous invisible worlds; the reality of dynamic reactions of all kinds triggered by the least human act; the reality of the transmigration of the self.
>
> Their ideal: permanence and stability.
>
> Their solution: withdraw from the external; sever all bonds with desires, loves, hates, ambitions, covetousness; remain in a state of immutable indifference.

The gospel tells us, to the contrary, that any living thing is precious because it is the work of God. God sows ceaselessly and multiplies life. And we must do the same within our small sphere. God does not act for himself, but for his creatures. We too must learn to live for others—and do so

THE CROWNING OF HIS WORK

as of now, immediately. Everything is real, there is no illusion in the absolute sense in which the Hindus understand *Maya*. Nothing belongs to us; hence we are held accountable for all our instruments and all the occasions to work God grants us. So we must not shirk any requests from circumstances or people. Finally, to want what is agreeable is natural, but the true will masters our inclinations and alone ennobles us, since it alone takes us out of ourselves. According to Christ, this victory over the self for the love of God and for our fellowman is the only veritable and salutary school of the will.

The Christian chooses among several possible actions: the one seemingly in conformity with the gospel; the one demanding the greatest mastery over the self; the one posing the greatest material difficulties. From then on, his action, no matter how humble it be, will become the freest of contingencies, the most universal in its consequences, the purest in its radiance, the most fertile in its vital possibilities. Such is the road to liberty.

By means of persevering exercises, we begin to conquer the material complications with greater and greater ease; we begin to control ourselves more and more easily; and little by little we form the habit of acting, of living, joyfully, with élan, with love of God and sympathy for our fellowman.

In practice, as it is intention (i.e., love) that animates action with a spiritual, more or less crystalline flame, one must primarily achieve the purest of love. Everything done in union with Christ partakes of his light. For instance, if a woman goes to a ball, regardless whether she goes for pleasure or to conform to conventions, for her this ball will be either a fall or a spiritualization. If the same woman rises early to run to a clinic in an impoverished district, whether

The Just Judge

she goes for show or for the love of her fellowman, her efforts will end either in a fall or a spiritualization. One can live with heaven in the worst surroundings, or one can live selfishly in a sanctimonious milieu. We must bring the sincerest and most impartial care to the examination and critique of our motives. Teeming as it is with ruses, the self strains untiringly to baffle our conscience. Generally speaking, we will never go astray if we accept all the tasks that come our way, whether they are common, heroic, lowly, or decorative. There where we live, there is where we must work.

Far from seeking an extraordinary life on a certain social level, or choosing non-conformities, the Christian will accept the fact that the advancement of his immortal being, the cultivation of his will, are possible everywhere. If we withdraw from the world seeking solitude under the pretext of detachment from its dangers, it is probable that laziness will seep in. A well-to-do young man who never has any material worries, whose days are entirely free for his studies, will work far less than another young man whose poverty-stricken family imposes upon him to earn his keep and who has only his nights to prepare his exams. No other recipe than gymnastics will develop muscles. No other recipe than struggle against the diverse forms of selfishness will develop our volitive force.

Our duty must come first. If it leaves us free time, we can rest, meditate, and pray. Our status, our profession, may have been imposed upon us by circumstances or by our choice; or heaven may have led certain exceptional individuals to it. No matter: wherever we are is the best setting for our development. Exercises devised by men, however wise or tested they may be, never possess the vital and fecund value of those to which our desires have compelled us. Solely the fulfillment of these duties permits our acquiring suppleness, presence of mind, a vigilant, constant, and full possession of all of our energies. This fulfillment alone holds the whole reality, all the live substance that will nourish our forces while maintaining them in harmony.

The Mystical Judgment

YOU REMEMBER THE PARABLE OF THE WISE VIRGINS and the foolish virgins. Now, the bridegroom is Christ himself; but who are the virgins, what are the lamps, the oil, the wedding feast, this midnight hour when one hears a cry?

Ruysbroeck the Admirable (1293–1381) consecrated one of his vertiginous books to explain this allegory, *L'Ornement des Noces spirituelles*.[5] Christ, as he informs us, comes to us through his incarnation, through grace in our hearts, through his judgments at our death, and at the judgment of humanity. His coming is effected in an incomprehensible manner, in accordance with both his divine nature and his human nature, by means of his humility, his charity, and his patience.

As for we human beings, Ruysbroeck, the old ecstatic of the Groenendael ("Green Valley"), says that we go to meet him by going towards God, by going towards our fellowman, and by going towards ourselves—as well as by practicing the virtues of humility, obedience, abdication of the will, patience, leniency, compassion, generosity, zeal, moderation, and purity.

---

[5] *The Splendor of the Spiritual Nuptials* by John van Ruysbroeck, 1293–1331, a Flemish mystical theologian.

The Just Judge

Collaborating within us to this end are the free-will that dwells within the concupiscent soul with its councilors; the reasonable soul with its judge, the conscience; the irascible soul, with the multitude of all of our other forces of action that follow suit.[6]

Our meeting (tryst) with the bridegroom may take place through the intentions at the back of our works, through repentance, or through annihilation of the self.

But in that deep dark night one must become clairvoyant; and one becomes so only thanks to the light of grace—by divesting ourselves of and rejecting all exterior images, and by the conversion of the will in which all forces are concentrated. The bridegroom enters us either through the ineffable action of heaven in the heart or in our concupiscent soul, either through the superior forces of the reasonable soul or in the unity of the Spirit.

Let us try to find a more positive meaning for this parable. We could, following the Unknown Philosopher,[7] speculate upon the remarkable virtues found in the number ten and the double quinary that play such an important role here. But we will better understand each other by setting aside the language of adepts. Heaven prefers its arcana to be within reach of everyone. First of all, certain circumstances of the story (such as the cortege, the lights, the nocturnal clamor) that become very important to symbolic interpretations are simply common customs at Jewish weddings. We need only focus on the simple web of the story. The

---

[6] See Littre: the ancient philosophers admitted that there were three faculties of the soul: the human (concupiscent), the irascible, and the reasonable.

[7] Louis-Claude de Saint-Martin.

mysterious bridegroom of the souls, the shepherd of the canticles, the Word, is preparing to celebrate his union with his servants whom he loves, and to whom he gives himself with beatitude. But a few of them were lacking in foresight; they had not acquired light, nor the means of feeding it, even though they possessed a lamp. It is too late. One cannot acquire merits except by day, during the activity of creation. When everything is at rest, nothing more may be attempted until the following day, or at least until the next nuptials. "Hence, work while the light is with you."

⊕

The parable of the wise virgins and the foolish virgins is recreated daily before our eyes. How do we act? Let us observe our actions by taking notice of our indolence, of our inattentiveness to God, and of the vitality of our selfishness. Do you notice in our relationships the inoperative Platonism of our mutual friendships, and the stiff-necked approach that prevents our souls from pouring from one into another; this aloofness that prevents us from exalting the ones for the sake of the others? Do you see the cause that prevents us from comforting the lassitude of others, from jolting the indifference of others on the outside?

This is because we swim in vagueness, too wrapped up in the irreality of our personal occupations, too imbedded in the nonchalance of our petty desires. We must at all costs look beyond and escape from our self-limitations, and with a definite aim in view—for otherwise, someday tough, cruel shepherds will press us forward not with crooks but with spikes.

See how much we have received! To balance a few episodes of melancholia, how many times of exaltation and

The Just Judge

inner joy have we not experienced? Moreover, whatever we or someone else have been able to do that was worthwhile was accomplished only because that force had been granted to us. We are constantly indebted to heaven, today more than ever. Our sole merit always lies in accepting that great gift from God.

Were we able to see the splendorous future that suffering prepares for us, how rapturously would we welcome this hard taskmaster, how much would we learn from its visit, how forcibly would we engage any ordeals! I cannot compel you to the mystical exploit, or to the secret conflagration of embracing the cross. I cannot even ask our Friend to predispose you towards it. You are free. You must choose; you you must decide for yourself. I can only repeat that verity, reality, and life are to be found therein.

I am well aware that we slumber during the night. But at least may the unique star of faith shine during that time, and may great gusts of love fill it with its fragrance. Buoyancy or cheerfulness is not to be found in things. It will dwell in our heart only after we have poured out its powerlessness and its slag into the incandescent heart of our Master, the only one who loves us perpetually.

We are weak as long as we lean on and depend solely upon ourselves; we remain lukewarm as long as we do not fan our flame; we are timorous only if we remain alone. Let us then lean on his almighty strength; let us carbonize our selfishness; let us cling to the mantle of the great Shepherd. He is never happier than when we importune him.

How many events have brought incalculable results because their seed, their roots, have been drenched with the purest blood of martyrs! A cup that is not emptied down to the dregs attracts other cups still more bitter. No torture of ours counts unless it removes one thorn from the head of Jesus—the perpetual martyr.

Let us rise to the level of circumstances. Let us forget ourselves. Let us become absorbed solely with the aim of alleviating the suffering of those who surround us. Have you not all verified that Jesus hears our prayers and grants them?

But for Jesus to hear you it does not suffice to seek him interiorly by desire, and by imploring him! Look for him out there, in the desolate regions where he proclaims himself to be sojourning—that is, wherever one finds suffering, tears, and despair. Let us always go towards the poor—the bodily ill, the poor in heart, the poor in spirit—even if we feel as poor as they. In a word, let us attempt the impossible, because the impossible is the domain of God.

The Sentence of the Judge

MATERIAL CHARITY IS THE INDISPENSABLE SCHOOL to all other kinds of charity. The physical plane is the humus—perhaps not too clean, but tonic—wherein all the sowings from the light find the aliment of its vital fire. Without the act, no inner refining is viable—it is neither salubrious nor harmonious. The act is the regulator of our energies, the foundation of the spiritual home, the fulcrum of the lever by means of which the mystic uplifts the world. The gesture of offering a piece of bread is not complete if the hand alone effects it. When I stated previously that to give of one's force to the one who is parched by the fire of anguish, to sustain with friendship the soul who feels foreign to the earth, to clothe a naked intelligence with concepts, to teach an ineffectual will the gymnastics of the will to strengthen it, to bring back a spirit that strays to the con-

The Just Judge

fines of the world in the sands wherein all verdure dies, without fear of fatigue or of wasting our time—so, when I was giving you these examples of the sole charitable deed that the Word recompenses, you understood that these are but diverse forms of the one and only offering.

Each act is a light emerging from within the self. The more energy we spend for that first act, the brighter the light; the deeper the center from which it gushed, the more pellucid is the light. Hence, to give moral force results in a beautifully hued star; to offer a glass of water to get rid of a tenacious, importunate beggar gives but a smoky glimmer; but to make the same pitiful gesture with the homogeneous concordance of all our faculties, with the total devotedness of our inner faculties in volitive unity and organic plenitude—so that its hidden irradiation must burst forth into the formal beauty of the gesture—that becomes a scintillating star! For true beauty is always the sign of a profound perfection, whereas prettiness is merely superficial.

We must also state that perfect almsgiving will be within our power only the day that harmony will equally have been perfected within us. Meanwhile, let us try to give as best we can; our ultimate effort will attract the gaze of the poor of God.

To see in the person of the debtor the Word himself is not a metaphysical artifice. All religious leaders have promulgated that teaching; but their commentators rendered it vapid.

Where there is suffering, there one finds the Word. What is suffering if not a death, a transformation, a cure, an excoriated individualism? And who can effect these things? Is it the moribund, the sick patient, or the selfish man? Is it not rather the Master of life, of health and love? Man has to

THE CROWNING OF HIS WORK

submit to his fate; but when his will exalts itself to heroic levels, his ultimate effort merely reaches acceptance and grief. And since dolor is but the sign of divine action upon us, the Word is always found behind us as the physician, as the remedy, as the very process of the healing.

Moreover, he has done, does now, and will continue doing more for us than what we can ever give in return to others, since what we give does not belong to us. By imitating him, we evoke him. He stands at our side ceaselessly as guide and witness. Hence, we must ultimately bring everything back to him, because the universe can truly become what we want it to be, not only according to our mental constructions, but also in its biology and in its vitalism.

If perchance our intention is not totally pure when we perform a kind act, it suffices that we give a thought of serving the Master, for him to welcome that act.

By identifying the unfortunate with the Word, we learn to respect dolor. The suffering one, the poor, is the theater of an admirable drama. We collaborate in that drama through our sympathy—we are subscribers, contributing to a work of general interest.

Let us make our offering with humility, with joy, love, and respect. Our spirit can then stand before the ineffable visage of the Savior, and the merit of our gesture remains integral because we understand that it is we who have become the debtor of the unfortunate, and that in fact we owe him thanks.

Such is the most rational meaning of the old Brahmanic lesson, "Leave behind the position of object, subject, and organ of perception; of the thing seen, eye, and brain; of the debtor, alms-giver, and donor"—through which the *chela* was elevated above the three great systems of ethics

The Just Judge

and of metaphysics. The saga of the cosmos thus appeared to him as a vast thought of divine intelligence that emanates beings from its unfathomable unity, analyzes them, scatters them to the very limits of the world, and reconstitutes them first by juxtaposition, then by syncretism, and finally by synthesis. Human meditation is, moreover, the image of divine meditation.

The eternal solicitude that brings all creatures ceaselessly back to the divine center is nothing but the cosmic function of the Word, of whom our Lord Jesus Christ in his dual nature is both the most concrete and the most comprehensible materialization to us.

CHAPTER III

The Faithful Friend

IT WAS SIX DAYS before Easter. Jesus went to Bethany where lived Lazarus whom he had brought back from the dead. There, a supper was prepared for him at the home of Simon the leper. Martha served and Lazarus was one of the guests. Then Mary went to fetch a pound of pure perfume of nard,[1] which was very expensive. She came in, bearing an alabaster vessel. While Jesus was at the table she broke the vessel and poured the perfume over his head. She also anointed Jesus's feet and wiped them with her hair. The house was filled with the smell of the perfume.

Seeing this, the disciples became indignant and said: "Why waste this perfume in this manner?" Judas the Iscariot, son of Simon, the one among the disciples who was to betray him, said: "It could have been sold very dearly! This perfume is worth more than three hundred denarii, which could have been given to the poor!" He said that, not that he was concerned about the poor, but because he was a thief, and, being in charge of the common funds, was stealing from what was being put into it. The disciples continued complaining about her, which Jesus noticed, and said: "Leave her alone! Why are you troubling this woman? She performed a good deed for my sake. The poor are always with you, and you can do good for them whenever you like; but you do not have me forever… She

---

[1] Nard is an aromatic flower of the lavender family, or the unguent made from it.

THE CROWNING OF HIS WORK

has done what she could. By pouring this perfume over my body, she has embalmed it in advance for my tomb. So I say unto you, verily, wherever this gospel of the kingdom shall be preached in the whole world, what she has done will also be spoken of in memory of her."

⊕

Then Satan entered Judas, known as the Iscariot, who was one of the Twelve. He went, to come to an agreement with the main sacrificers and officers about what had to be done to deliver Jesus to them. He said to them: "What will you give me if I deliver him up to you?" At these words, they were filled with joy. They agreed to pay him, and gave him thirty pieces of silver. So he gave his promise. From that time on he looked for a suitable occasion to deliver him to them when there would not be a crowd.

⊕

A large crowd of Jews had learned that Jesus was in Bethany. They hurried there not only because of him but also to see Lazarus, whom he had raised from the dead. So the chief priests began thinking of having Lazarus killed, for a great number of Jews were abandoning them because of this man, and believing in Jesus. The next day, a large crowd, which had come to the festival, having been informed that Jesus was coming to Jerusalem, went out to meet him. As he was approaching Bethphage, near the mountain known as the Mount of Olives, Jesus sent two of the disciples,

The Faithful Friend

saying: "Go to the hamlet that is before you; as you go in, you will find a she-ass tied up with her foal on which no man has ever sat; untie it and bring it. If anyone asks you: 'Why are you untying it?' you will reply: 'The Lord has need of it,' and at that moment they will let it go."

The messengers left and found the foal of the ass, as he had told them, tied up outside near a gate at the side of the road. While they were untying it, its masters said: "What are you doing, why are you untying that young-ass?" They replied: "Because the Lord has need of it." And they were allowed to go.

In all these things, the word of the prophet was being fulfilled:

Say to the daughter of Zion:
See, your King is coming to you
Gentle, and mounted on an ass,
On a foal, on the young of a beast of burden.

So the disciples led the young-ass to Jesus. They threw their coats over the young-ass and had Jesus mount it. When he was on his way, many people spread their cloaks on the road, others strewed branches they had cut in the fields; a great many had palm branches in their hands. As he was about to reach the downward slope of the Mount of Olives, the multitude of disciples, in transports of joy, began to praise God aloud for all the miracles they had seen. They kept saying: "Blessed be the King who comes in the name of the Lord! Peace in the heavens! Glory in the highest places!" The crowds who had gone before, and those who followed, acclaimed him: "Hosanna to the Son of David! Hosanna to the king of Israel! Blessed be the reign which is coming, the reign of David our father! Peace in heaven and glory in the highest places!" At first, his disciples could not understand these things. But when Jesus had been glorified, they remembered that they had been written about him, and that it was they themselves who had fulfilled them with regard to him.

However, the crowd which was with him when he had called Lazarus forth from the grave and brought him back from the dead gave witness to him. It was also because they had learned that it was he who had performed this miracle that the multitude had come to meet him. Thereupon the Pharisees were saying to one another: "You see that you are gaining nothing; see how everyone is running after him." So some of the Pharisees who were in the crowd said to Jesus: "Master, silence your disciples!" "I say unto you," replied Jesus, "if these men keep quiet, the stones will cry out!"

As he was approaching the town and it appeared before him, he wept over it, saying: "Oh! if only you could have understood, at least today, what could have brought you peace! But all of this now remains hidden from your eyes. Days will come for you when your enemies will surround you with an entrenchment and will enclose you and close in on you from all sides; they will totally destroy you and your children in your midst, and they will not leave stone upon stone within you, because you did not realize the time you were visited!"

The Faithful Friend

When he entered Jerusalem, the whole town was moved. They were saying: "Who is this man?" But the crowds replied: "This man? This is the prophet, Jesus of Nazareth in Galilee!"

⊕

The next morning, as they had left Bethany, going back to the town, Jesus became hungry. He sighted from afar on the edge of the road a solitary fig-tree which had leaves, so he went to see whether he would find any fruit there. When he had come close, he found nothing but leaves, for it was not the fig season. So, speaking to the tree, he said to it: "May no one ever eat of your fruit again!" And the disciples heard these words.

When they had reached Jerusalem, Jesus entered the temple and began to chase away the sellers and buyers. He overturned the tables of the money-changers and the seats of the dove sellers. He could not even bear anyone to carry an implement across the temple. He was teaching and saying: "Is it not written: 'My house will be called a house of prayer, for all the nations.' And you have made it into a den of thieves!"

Upon hearing these words, the scribes, the main sacrificers, and the chiefs of the people sought by what means they would make him die; for they feared him because the whole crowd admired his doctrine.

Then some blind and some lame people came up to him in the temple, and he healed them.

THE CROWNING OF HIS WORK

But the main sacrificers and the scribes, seeing the wonders he was performing upon hearing the children who were crying out in the temple "Hosanna to the son of David!" became indignant. They said to him: "Do you hear what these people are saying?" "Yes," Jesus answered them, "and you, have you ever read: 'Out of the mouths of little children, of sucklings, you prepared praises for yourself?'"

They did not know what to do to eradicate him, for the whole populace hung upon his every word.

Even though he had performed so many miracles before them, they did not believe in him. Thus were the words of Isaiah the prophet fulfilled: "Lord, who has believed in our preaching? To whom has the hand of the Lord been revealed?" Even then they still could not believe, because Isaiah further said: "He has blinded their eyes and hardened their hearts, for fear that they might see with their eyes and understand with their hearts, that they be converted and that I heal them!" Isaiah said these things when he saw the glory of the Lord and that he spoke of him.

However, there were several, even among the chiefs, who believed in Jesus; but because of the Pharisees they did not admit it, for fear of being driven out of the synagogue. For they loved the glorification that comes from men more than the glory that comes from God.

The Faithful Friend

That is why Jesus raised his voice and cried: "Whoever believes in me does not believe in me, but in him who sent me. I, who am the light, I came into the world so that whoever believes in me shall not remain in darkness. As for him who hears my words and does not keep them, it is not I who judges him; for I have not come to judge the world, but to save the world. Whoever rejects me and does not receive my words already has his judge; this judge is the very word I have spoken, which shall judge on the last day. For I have not spoken of my own accord, but it is the Father, whose messenger I am, who has himself commanded me to speak, and has prescribed what I had to say. And I know that his commandment is eternal life. Therefore, the things that I say are just said as the Father has said them to me."

As the evening had come, Jesus left them and went out of the town to go to Bethany, where he spent the night.

⊕

In the morning, as they were returning to the town, the disciples saw the fig-tree dried up even to the roots. Peter, remembering, said to Jesus: "Master, see: the fig-tree you cursed has dried up!"

The disciples were astonished at this. How could this fig-tree have dried up all of a sudden? Then Jesus, addressing everyone, declared: "Have faith in God. Verily, I say unto you, if you had faith and had no doubt at all, not only would you do what has been done to the fig-tree, but were you to say to this very

THE CROWNING OF HIS WORK

mountain, without having any doubt in your heart: 'Move from here and cast yourself into the sea!' it would be fulfilled. That is why I am telling you: All that you ask in prayer, believe that you shall receive it, and it shall be granted unto you."

"When you say your prayers, if you have anything against anyone, forgive, so that your Father who is in heaven shall also forgive your sins."

⊕

Among those who had come to worship God during the feast were some Greeks. They approached Philip who was from Bethsaida in Galilee, and made this request: "Lord, we wish to see Jesus." Philip went to tell Andrew, and together they both went to tell Jesus. He then addressed the following words to them: "The hour has come when the Son of Man must be glorified. Verily, I say unto you, if the grain of wheat that has fallen to the ground does not undergo death, it remains alone; but were it to die, it would bear many fruits. Whoever loves his life shall lose it; and whoever hates his life in this world shall keep it for eternal life. Let him who wishes to serve me follow me! And wherever I am, my servant shall be also. If someone serves me, my Father will honor him. Now my soul is troubled; but what shall I say? Shall I say: Father, save me from this hour? Yet it is for this hour that I have come. Father, may your name be glorified." Then from the heavens there came a voice: "I have glorified him and I shall glorify him again!" "It is thunder" said the crowd

The Faithful Friend

which was there and heard. There were some who said: "It is an angel who has spoken to him."

Jesus continued thus: "It is not for me but for you that this voice has sounded. The judgment of this world is now taking place; the prince of this world shall now be driven out; and when I am raised from this earth, I shall draw all men to me." He said this to indicate the kind of death he was going to undergo.

The crowd answered him: "The Law teaches us that the Christ lives eternally; then how can you say: 'The Son of Man must be raised from the earth.' Who is this Son of Man?" Jesus answered them: "The light is among you for still a little while. Walk while you still have light, for fear that the darkness shall overtake you. He who walks in darkness does not know whither he is going. While you have light, believe in the light, in order to become sons of light." Thus Jesus spoke, then he went away and hid from them.

As he had loved his people who were in the world, before the feast of the Passover, knowing that the time had come for him to pass from this world to the Father, Jesus gave them a supreme sign of love. During the supper (the devil having already put into the heart of Judas the Iscariot, son of Simon, to betray him), Jesus, who knew that the Father had put everything into his hands, that he had come from God and that he was going to God, got up from the table, took off his garment, and having taken a cloth, wrapped it around him. Then he filled the bowl with water and

THE CROWNING OF HIS WORK

began to wash the feet of his disciples and to wipe them with the cloth he had wrapped around him. Then he came to Simon Peter who said to him: "Lord, you would wash my feet!" Jesus answered him: "You do not know now what I am doing, but you shall understand later on." Peter said to him: "You shall never wash my feet!" Jesus answered him: "If I do not wash you, you shall have no part in me." Simon Peter told him: "Lord, not only my feet, but also my hands and my head!" Jesus answered: "Whoever has bathed needs only to wash his feet; he is completely pure. Now, you are pure, but not all of you." For he knew which one it was who would betray him; that is why he said "All of you are not pure."

After having washed their feet, he took up his garment and, having sat down at the table once more, he said to them "Do you understand what I have done to you? You call me Master and Lord, and you are right to do so, for that I am. Therefore, if I who am the Lord and Master have washed your feet, you must wash each other's feet. For I have given you an example so that you will do as I have done to you.

When Jesus had spoken thus, he was troubled in his mind and said openly: "Verily, verily I declare unto you, one of you, who is eating with me, shall betray me!" The disciples looked at one another, asking themselves anxiously which one he was referring to. They were deeply saddened; each of them began asking him "Lord, is it I?"

The Faithful Friend

The one who was seated next to Jesus was he whom Jesus loved. Simon Peter beckoned him and asked: "Tell me, whom is he speaking of?" This disciple, having immediately leaned over Jesus's breast, asked him "Lord, who is it?" "It is he," replied Jesus, "to whom I shall give this piece of bread which I am going to dip." And Jesus, dipping a piece, gave it to Judas son of Simon, the Iscariot.

As soon as Judas had taken it, Satan entered him. Jesus told him: "Do what you intend to do without delay." None of those who were at the table understood why he was saying that to him. Some thought that, as Judas had the purse, Jesus was telling him: "Buy what we need for the feast," or "Give something to the poor." As soon as Judas had taken the piece of bread, he left abruptly. It was dark.

When Judas had gone out, Jesus said: "The one who put his hand into the dish with me is the one who will hand me over. As for the Son of Man, he is going away according to what is written about him; but woe unto that man through whom the Son of Man is delivered! It would be better for that man if he had never been born!

"Now the Son of Man has been glorified, and God has been glorified in him. If God has been glorified in him, God himself in his turn shall glorify him, and he shall glorify him soon.

THE CROWNING OF HIS WORK

"My little children, I am still with you for a little while. You will look for me and, as I have said to the Jews, I am also telling you: you cannot go where I am going.

"I am giving you a new commandment: love one another; as I have loved you, love one another. This is how everyone shall know that you are my disciples, if you have love for one another." "Lord," asked Simon Peter, "where are you going to?" "Where I am going," Jesus answered him, "you cannot follow me now, but you shall follow me later."

"Let not your heart be troubled; you believe in God, believe also in me. There are several mansions in my Father's house; if not, I would have told you. I am going to prepare a place for you; and when I have gone and shall have prepared you a place, I shall come back and I shall take you with me, so that wherever I am you shall be also. And you know the path to the place where I am going."

Thomas asked him: "Lord, we do not know where you are going, how could we know the way?" Jesus told him "I am the way, the truth, and the life; no one comes to the Father but through me. If you knew me, you would know my Father also, and as of now, you know him and have seen him." Philip said to him: "Lord, show us the Father and that will be sufficient for us." Jesus answered: "I have been with you for such a long time, yet you do not know me, Philip! Whoever has seen me has seen the Father. How can you say: 'Show us the Father'? Do you not believe that I am in the Father and that the Father is in me? It is not by myself that I speak the words that I am saying to you. It is the Father, dwelling within me, who performs these works. Believe me, believe that I am in the Father and that the Father is in me; or at least believe because of these works themselves.

"Verily, verily I say unto you, whoever believes in me shall also perform the works that I perform, and he shall do greater things, because I am going to the Father; and whatever you ask in my name, I shall do it, so that the Father may be glorified in the Son. If you ask something in my name, I shall do it. If you love me, keep my commandments, and I shall pray to the Father. Then he shall give you another Consoler who shall always be with you, the Spirit of Truth, whom the world cannot receive, for it neither sees nor does it know him, but you, you know him because he dwells with you and he will be within you.

"I shall not leave you as orphans, I shall come back to you. In a very short time the world shall see me no more; but you shall see me. Because I am living, you too shall live. On that day, you will know that I am in my Father, that you are in me, and that I am in you. Whoever keeps my commandments and follows them, that is who loves me. And whoever loves me shall be loved by my Father, and I shall love him and manifest myself unto him."

THE CROWNING OF HIS WORK

Jude (not to be confused with Judas, the Iscariot) asked him: "Lord, how is it that you shall manifest yourself to us and not to the world?" Jesus answered him: "If somebody loves me, he will keep my word and my Father shall love him and we shall come to him and we shall take up our abode with him. Whoever does not love me does not keep my word; and the word you hear is not from me but from him who has sent me—from the Father. I am telling you all of that while I am still among you; but the Consoler, the Holy Spirit, whom the Father shall send in my name, shall teach you all things and remind you of all that I have taught you. I am leaving you peace, I am giving you my peace; I am not giving it to you as the world gives it; let not your heart be troubled, let it not weaken. You have heard what I have told you: I am going away and I am coming back to you. If you loved me, you would rejoice that I am going to the Father, because the Father is greater than I am. Therefore I have spoken to you before the event, so that you might believe when it happens. I shall seldom speak to you any more, for the prince of this world is coming; he has nothing of me; but he is coming so that the world may know that I love the Father and that I am acting according to the orders of the Father. Let us get up and go from here."

⊕

"I am the true vine, and my Father is the vine-grower. Every stem in me that does not bear fruit he cuts off. And every stem which bears, he prunes so that it may

The Faithful Friend

bear even more. You are already trimmed because of the words which I have imparted to you...

"Abide in me and I shall abide in you. Just as the stem cannot bear fruit by itself though it must remain attached to the vine, neither can you bear any if you do not abide in me. I am the vine; you are the vine-stems. Whoever abides in me and in whom I abide brings forth many fruits, because outside of me you can do nothing. If somebody does not abide in me, he is cast out like the vine-stem and he dries up, and this stem is gathered up and it is thrown into the fire and it burns. If you abide in me, and if my words abide in you, whatever you would like, ask for it and you shall receive it. My Father is glorified in that you bear many fruits and then shall you become my disciples. As the Father has loved me, so have I loved you; abide in my love. If you keep my commandments, you shall abide in my love; as I have kept the commandments of my Father so I abide in his love. I have spoken to you in this way so that my joy may be yours, and that your joy may become plenitude.

"This is my commandment: love one another as I have loved you. No love is greater than the love of one who gives his life for his friends. You are my friends if you do as I command you. I no longer call you servants, for the servant does not know what his master does. I have called you my friends, because I have made known to you all that I have learned from my Father. It is not you who have chosen me; it is I who have chosen you and have put you in your place so that you may bear fruit and that your fruit may remain; then all that you ask of the Father in my name, that shall he give unto you. What I am commanding you to do is to love one another.

"If the world hates you, know that it has hated me before it hated you. If you were of the world, the world would love you because you would belong to it; since you are not of the world, as I have chosen you from the world, because of this the world hates you. Remember the word I have told you: the servant is not greater than his master. As they have persecuted me, so shall they persecute you; if they have kept my word, so shall they keep yours. But all of these things they shall do to you, because of my name, because they do not know him who has sent me.

"If I had not come, and if I had not spoken to them at all, they would not be guilty; but now their guilt is without excuse. He who hates me also hates my Father. If I had not performed works in their midst which no other had done, they would not be guilty; but now they have seen them, and nevertheless they have hated both me and my Father; but it is so, that the word written in their Law shall be accomplished: they hated me without cause. When the Comforter comes, whom I am sending you on behalf of the Father, the Spirit of Truth who also proceeds from the Father, shall bear witness to me; and you also shall bear me witness, for you have been with me from the beginning.

"I have told you this, that you may be spared any downfall. They shall chase you out of the synagogues, even the hour is coming when whoever shall kill you

The Faithful Friend

shall believe he is worshipping God. And they shall act in this way because they have known neither the Father nor me. But I have told you these things so that when the hour has come you shall remember that I have told them to you. I did not tell them from the beginning, because I was with you. Now I am going to the One who has sent me, yet none of you asks me: 'Where are you going?' But because I have told you that, sadness has filled your heart. However, I am telling you the truth. It is good for you that I am going away, for if I do not go away the Comforter will not come to you at all; but if I go away, I shall send him to you. And when he comes, he will convince the world of sin, righteousness, and judgment: of sin, because men do not believe in me; of righteousness, because I am going to the Father and because you shall see me no more; of judgment, because the prince of this world is judged.

"I have many more things to tell you, but they are now beyond your reach. When the Spirit of Truth has come, he will guide you to the whole truth, for he will not speak on his own authority but will say everything he has heard, and he will impart to you the things to come. It is he who will glorify me, because he will take of what is mine and shall impart it to you. Everything which the Father has is mine, that is why I have said that he shall take of what is mine and that he shall impart to you.

"In a little while, you shall see me no more; then, after a little while, you shall see me, because I am going to the Father." Then some of his disciples said to one another: "What did he say to us: 'In a little while and you shall see me no more; then again, in a little while and you shall see me'; and 'because I am going to the Father?' So they were saying: a little while? We do not know what he is talking about."

Jesus, realizing that they wanted to question him, told them: "You are asking one another what these words mean: In a little while and you shall not see me; then a little while later you shall see me. Verily, verily, I said unto you, you shall cry and you shall lament and the world will rejoice; you will be doleful, but your sadness will be turned into joy. When a woman is in labor, she is in pain because her hour has come; but when the child is born, she no longer remembers her anguish in the joy she feels that a man is born into the world. Similarly, you are now in pain, but I shall you see again, and your heart will rejoice, and nobody shall take your joy away from you. On that day, you will no longer question me about anything. Verily, verily I say this to you, that whatever you shall ask the Father for, he shall give it to you in my name. Until now, you have not asked for anything in my name; ask and you shall receive, so that your joy may be perfect.

"I have told you these things in proverbs; the hour is coming when I shall no longer speak to you in proverbs, but when I shall speak openly to you about the Father. On that day you will ask in my name, and I am not telling you that I will pray to the Father for you, for the Father himself loves you because you have loved me, and that you believed that I came on behalf of the Father. I came forth from the Father and I have

The Faithful Friend

come into this world; now I am leaving this world and I am going to the Father."

His disciples said to him: "It is now that you are speaking openly and that you are not speaking in proverbs. Now we know that you know all things and that you do not need anybody to question you; that is why we believe you came from God." Jesus answered them: "Now you believe! See, the hour is coming and it has already come when you shall be dispersed, each one to his own place, and when you shall leave me alone; but I am not alone, because the Father is with me. I have spoken to you in this way so that you shall have peace in me. You shall have tribulations in the world; but take courage, I have conquered the world."

⊕

Jesus spoke thus; then, lifting his eyes to the heavens, he said: "Father, the hour has come; glorify your Son so that your Son may glorify you and, by the power you have given him over all flesh, he may give eternal life to all those whom you have given to him. This is eternal life, that they may know you, you the only true God, and him whom you have sent, Jesus Christ.

"I have glorified you on earth; I have fulfilled the work you have given me to do. And now, glorify me, Oh Father, close by your side, with the glory I had with you before the world was.

"I have revealed your name to the men you have given me in the world. They were yours, you gave them to me and they have kept your word. Now, they have recognized that everything you have given me comes from you. The words you gave me, I have given to them, and they have received them, and they have truly recognized that I came from you, and they have believed that it is you who have sent me.

"It is for them that I pray; it is not for the world that I pray, but for those whom you have given me, because they are yours (for all that is mine is yours and all that is yours is mine) and because I am glorified in them. I am no longer in the world, but they are in the world, and I am coming to you Holy Father! Keep them in your name, the name that you have given me, so that they may be one as we are one. When I was with them it was I who kept them in your name, the name which you gave me, and I have preserved them, and none of them was lost, except the son of perdition, so that the Scripture would be fulfilled. Now I am coming to you, and I am speaking thus, for I am still in the world, that they may have the plenitude of my joy within them.

"I have given them your word, and the world has hated them because they are not of the world as I am not of the world. I do not ask you to take them out of the world, but that you preserve them from evil. They are not of the world, just as I am not of the world. Sanctify them through the truth; your word is truth.

"Just as you have sent me into the world, I also have sent them into the world, and I sanctify myself for them so that they too may be sanctified by the truth. It is not only for them that I am praying, but also for those who shall believe in me through their word, so

The Faithful Friend

that they may all be one, as you, Father, are in me and I am in you, that they too may be in us, so that the world may believe that it is you who have sent me. And the glory you have given to me I have given to them, so that they may be one as we are one, I in them and you in me, that this unity may be perfect and the world may recognize that it is you who have sent me and that you have loved them as you have loved me.

"Father! My desire is that wherever I am, those whom you have given me may be there with me, that they may see the glory that you have given me, because you loved me before the creation of the world. Righteous Father! the world has not known you; but I have known you and so these people have recognized that it is you who have sent me. I have made your name known to them; and I shall make them know it, so that the love with which you have loved me may be in them and that I, too, may be in them."

The day of the feast came, the first day of unleavened bread, when the Passover lamb was being sacrificed. The disciples asked Jesus: "Where do you want us to go to prepare the Passover meal for you?"

So he sent Peter and John. "Go," he told them; "as you enter the town, you will see a man carrying a jar of water; follow him into the house he enters. You shall say to the owner: 'The Master wants it to be said to you: "My time is near; it is with you that I must eat the Passover with my disciples." Where is the room in which I shall celebrate it?' He will show you a large upper room with table covers, all ready. Make the preparations there."

The disciples left. They came into the town and found the things just as Jesus had told them; and they prepared the Passover.

While they were eating, Jesus took some bread, and having said the blessing, he broke it and gave it to the disciples, saying: "Take, eat, this is my body which is given for you, do this in memory of me." Then, after the supper, he took the cup and gave thanks, gave it to them and said: "Drink of it all of you, this is my blood, the blood of the new testament, which, on behalf of many, is shed for the remission of sins. And from now on, I say to you, I shall no longer drink of this fruit of the vine until that day when I shall drink with you, anew, in my Father's kingdom."[2]

The Victory of Ascendant Love

LET US VISUALIZE A CEREMONIAL REPAST AT THE HOME of a wealthy Israelite. Simon, in whose house this feast was being given, belonged to the rich and self-righteous upper class. In this traditional, intolerant, and snobbish milieu,

---

[2] John 12:1–11; Matt. 26:6–13; Mark 14:3–9; Matt. 26:14–16; Mark 14:10–11; Luke 22:3–6; John 12:12–19; Matt. 21:1–11; Mark 11:1–10; Luke 19:29–44; Matt. 21:12–17; Mark 11:15–18; Luke 19:45–48; John 2:14–17; Matt. 21:18–22; Mark 11:12–14; Mark 19–25; John 12:20–36; John 13:1–15; John 13:21–30; Matt. 26:20–25; Mark 14:17–21; Luke 22:21–23; John 13:31–36; John 14; John 15; John 16; John 17; Matt. 26:17–19; Mark 14:12–16; Luke 22:7–13; Matt. 26:26–29; Mark 14:22–25; Luke 22:14–23.

The Faithful Friend

how scandalous and astonishing it must have been to see a woman coming towards the guest of honor to render him the startling homage that Mary Magdalene did, and especially to note that this rabbi, this prophet almost, accepted this woman's bold gesture and made use of it as a means to teach his uncompromising hosts a lesson! We must also think about the effort this modest sister of Lazarus must have made to dare undertake so outrageous and unheard of an act in the context of Judaic customs.

It is the extraordinary part of her act that has made her famous. Christ made use of it to establish the character of his teaching regarding womanhood. In the history of societies, instead of mutual agreement one notices much conflict between the sexes, with oppression over the weaker, polyandry being linked to matriarchy and polygamy to patriarchy. Whatever anti-clericals may say, Christianity has done a great deal to hasten social equilibrium between man and woman, no matter how far the councils of the Middle Ages erred. Feminism is emerging today, and we can only hope that the medley of somewhat ridiculous exaggerations on the one hand, and wise desiderata on the other, will come to be further clarified with time. Its most intuitive partisans have never told themselves that if today they are born as women, it is because their immortal spirit has so chosen to be. In reality, there is no "spiritualist" feminism; or, at least, its feminine "representatives" are for the most part unaware that "spiritualists" are sacrificial by nature. Were they aware of this, they would be happy to have been born women.

One can truly believe this to have been Jesus's sentiment, since he showed such respect, and later such affection, for a creature who in that era was an outcast of society.

THE CROWNING OF HIS WORK

One cannot repeat often enough that man and woman are not opposites, but complementaries. We need not invoke Brahmanic teachings to discover this evident law, according to which if, corporeally, man is active and woman passive, intellectually woman becomes active and man passive. Just as there is no physical generation without a man and a woman, neither is there an intellectual generation without a woman and a man. But on both planes, the role of the man is outer and that of the woman inner.

The hearth, the home, is a temple; and it is through the soul of the wife, the spouse, that intuitions and invisible presences enter therein. Her role as inspirer and consoler implies the most upright moral principle, but also the most acute sufferings. In any case, man would not outwardly appear to be the head of the family or the leader in civic life had not God permitted him to be.

The methods by which humankind has hitherto felt, learned, thought, and invented, have almost always been illicit. For we have devoted to the realization of desires (even if, perhaps, noble ones) forces that should first have served to do the will of heaven. To satisfy our aspirations is wrong if our motive is selfish, which is what happens most of the time. The inventor, the artist, and the scientist, who do not work primarily for God, no matter how universal and sublime their work may seem, are in fact, from a mystical point of view, merely bartering with their own god. They sell themselves to receive in return fortune, glory, or the joy of self-satisfying personal pride.

However, this inner polytheism is still preferable to atheism. Everyone cannot with one flick of the wings traverse the universe to land upon the summits of the Absolute; one has first to form one's wings.

The Faithful Friend

Many utilitarian philosophers would willingly be of the same opinion as Judas: that it is entirely unreasonable to waste so much money on so costly a perfume, when a great many poor people might have profited from the money so spent. In that case, nature is a prodigious wastrel! How many times has the Father again given us the same gifts before we began utilizing them? Had he been parsimonious with his patience, what would we have become? Let us also choose to be generous in extraordinary circumstances, for heaven does not demand asceticism. A rich man who gives everything away would renounce many pleasures, but would as well be released from many worries.

What we must be rid of is the feeling of possessiveness. We must maintain our status except in exceptional cases. It is more difficult to remain simple and good, rich than poor. The one who was born wealthy has authority; he can lord it over his servants, his subalterns and workmen; he can train them, educate them, help them; he can do much for domestic animals, for the earth, and his domains. In many circumstances he can participate in social redress, public life; he can conciliate, prevent evil, and better others' life conditions.

A man is not born in a specific family without profound reasons and without important goals. If of his own volition he leaves the post where God has placed him, it should be in order to undertake some more difficult task, not an easier one; moreover, he must make certain not to fail. Look at the precautions taken by all who choose exceptional paths. During their training, ascetics from India and Western monks accumulate guarantees from their most minute observances. They are all too well aware that the game of life puts us in touch only with persons and things with whom

THE CROWNING OF HIS WORK

we are personally involved—whether to make amends, to settle an old account, to give help, or to teach them something that someone else would be unable to do as well. Everything is solemn. Our humility must be profound, our confidence in God must be very solid for us to dare change our destiny of our own volition without falling into abysmal error. Thus, just as Mary Magdalene dared her utmost to prove her love, each of us in our own circumstances must likewise dare everything as an expression of verity.

To this purpose, speech is the means most generally employed. Yet how many efforts are needed for our discourse to bear fruits! First of all, our mouths must unlearn telling lies. A false word always kills something—in us, in the interlocutor, or in the secondary atmosphere. In these three settings an idle word is a waste, a squandering. Writing is still more exacting and potent. I am not concerned here with the profession or the technical baggage that the orator or literary man must acquire beforehand, the acquisition of which demands years of study. There is more to it than that.

Any relationship with our fellowmen is a sort of equation between the subject one treats, the conception one has of it, the chosen mode of expression, the state of the ambience, and the receptive capacity of the intended public.

The protagonist of an idea believes he chose it freely, when in reality he did nothing but receive, among all the splendors of the good and of truth, the one most adequate to his comprehension and to his spiritual understanding. This occurs entirely outside of his will. I mean to say that Titian became a painter and Bach a musician because within each existed a direct relationship with the invisible kingdom of color or with that of sound.

The Faithful Friend

But it is in the second state of our equation that human effort begins. Within us, we must prepare an apartment for our inborn intuition—whether it be scientific, philosophical, aesthetic, or religious. This is where moral culture plays its role. The purer our heart is, the better does light thrive therein. So, it is in depth that we must realize that the light of the Word comprises all lights, all sciences, all abstractions, all the beauty in form, color, and harmony, as well as the whole power of radiation. The more solid is our spiritual health, the more perfect is the external state of health of our intelligence, of our sensibility, and of our body. It is for this reason that we are required to maintain neat and clean the secret chambers of our inner palaces. Remember that within us there are palaces, magnificences, transplendencies of the dawn, devouring flames, and storms. These we obtain through our constancy in righteous reasoning, in nurturing beautiful thoughts, and in acting piously. Sweeping all prejudices aside, exterminating the vermin of selfishness, offering our invisible visitors to breathe the purest incense of our enthusiasms—thus do we facilitate our heart's access to the light that this constant moral effort forces to descend into our heart, and that we receive thereby in full plenitude.

Such is the formula of the tacit pact that any protagonist concludes with the truth he hopes to impart. Once the center is clear, the rest becomes pure.

It is essential, moreover, to take any accessory or specialized precautions required in view of the organ one employs. These precautions specifically mean: for the orator, no lies, no useless words, no base actions; for the writer, no personal polemics, no stingy thoughts, no vacuous reading matter; for the artist, no biased or warped sentiments, no

THE CROWNING OF HIS WORK

servile realism, no sensual slavery—and for all, a flaming desire for the best, for the optimum.

To acquire mastery over the skills required by our chosen profession demands a persevering will covering our craft, our trade—its rich vocabulary, alternating phases, design elements of color, of orchestration, etc. These things can be learned by utilizing our mental qualities. To that end there are schools, tradition, and the furtherance of our education on a personal basis.

In this connection, however, the role of environmental elements is a far lesser known factor, for all of its features abide in the invisible plane and reveal themselves only through signs, which must be most delicately interpreted. Among these signs are those that, before undertaking anything decisive, the ancients sought to interpret by means of omens, whether earthly or in the stars. But no matter how admirable their ordinance may be, divinatory sciences (whether in China or in India) only ever reveal but one corner of the mystery of things. We Christians step past this cavernous path that leads to polytheism. Having once amassed all the elements of the known, our gesture must be to turn towards the unknown with the tremulous supplication of prayer and the audacious certitude of faith.

As to the public, whether auditor or spectator, one can do nothing to prepare them.[3] Before two interlocutors meet face to face, they carry within themselves already the capacity of reciprocal understanding. Each seeks and goes where his thirst impels him. One can enjoy something from the supernatural only after having exhausted the acerbities of

---

[3] Although the Wagnerian scenic arrangements revived from the Brahmans, Egyptians, and Chaldeans allege the opposite.

The Faithful Friend

the temporal realm. Only those who have received a gift from God may hope that their words will bear durable fruits. Yes, the others may move us, but it will be impossible for them to change a heart, to transmute a spirit, or to regenerate a body. The only information available to most people is the silent contagion of example.

A good example is a light definitively acclimated to the here-below. The meditations that prepare for a good life, the soul sufferings that animate it, the physical fatigues one endures to realize one's duty—all these are phases through which the adaptation of an ideal to earthly conditions must pass. A light thus nurtured, clothed, or materialized will be understood by our fellowmen because it will have been formed by an act rather than having remained a concept or an aesthetic notion. If that light directs our conduct in all its phases, it will radiate from our presence. As spirit, it will speak to the spirits. Gushing from the depths of our heart, it will reach the bottom of hearts, will implant itself therein, and will help them in an efficacious and mysterious manner. This is the smoothest, the most fruitful, means to pass information along.

None of this demands special gifts or heroic efforts. What is essential is that we render what we have personally assimilated comprehensible to others. Let us look at this more closely.

Between the inner conception of an idea and its outer realization lies the domain of expression. Each of these three phases—corresponding, respectively, to the discovery of truth, the formation of the beautiful, and the action of good—possess their own organs, the first of which are susceptible to the principles of spiritual hygiene, the second to psychic hygiene, and the last to physiological hygiene.

THE CROWNING OF HIS WORK

Concepts are refined through moral discipline. Acts are perfected through physical disciplines or training. As to the intermediate stage of expression, it depends upon the relation of the spirit with matter, and of the organ with the surroundings.

All of these things were well-known to the ancients. They had a certain degree of knowledge (incomplete in itself, but profound in comparison to ours) of the links that unite corporeal beings to the dynamic invisible entities. In the temples are found all the texts useful for training the spiritual researcher, the philosopher, the poet, the musician, the orator, and the thaumaturgist. The results they obtained were ameliorations, improvements, and sublimations. What the gospel permits us to accomplish are veritable creations, because the disciple is an evocator of the absolute, a theurgist of the one God, and not of the gods anymore.

For him, the armies of beings exist merely as divine representations. He expects nothing from them and asks nothing of them. Having found refuge in God, standing at the right of Christ, he remains closely bound to him. No created splendor dazzles his sight, but he is ready to give of himself to any being, whether it be a pebble or a constellation, since each being is the object of Christ's providential tenderness.

Hence, waste no opportunity to do good; the invisible (which the Taoists call "wandering influences") is an exceedingly complicated mechanism. As inextricable as it can be on the physical plane, the intermingling of individuals, events, and forms is much more so on the other side of the veil—since perceptible events constitute but an infinitesimal part of the latent possibilities of the universe. Life on earth is a favor; spirits *en masse* press at the gates of this

The Faithful Friend

world in spite of the sufferings that await them—or rather, because of them.

By being scrupulously attentive, then, we practice benevolence on a broad scale. A great many people will benefit from our acts, from our sentiments, from our thoughts, because the higher is our ideal, the purer is our intention. To give in order to acquire merits is selfishness; to give through compassion is perfect—we can do no better. Later, when we will have learned to give everything, even our whole life, we will begin to think of acting from pure love of God; but it is useless to try that for the time being.

The Effort of Descendant Love

ANY SUFFERING, EVEN EXPIATORY SUFFERING, GENERates a light; it is a force that terminates its trajectory, an unknown that becomes integrated, a portion of the world that enters again into the equilibrium of healthiness. When the suffering is endured by an innocent person, there is all the more reason for the light emanating from it to be divine.

On the other hand, any organism is limited because it is material. Rather in the manner of a pitiless horseman, the spirit animating it wears it out and kills it—and this death is resolved into a rebirth, which is a blessing.

The particular esoteric teaching that attempts to defend and preserve the physical envelope from the reach of death is an arrogant error. It may attain its purpose only at the price of veritable assassinations which are that much the more criminal because in this case the murderer is operating under the cloak of mystery. Do not let promissory phrases dazzle you with their subtle thoughts or thaumaturgical exhibitions. Rather, take pains to discover the spirit

THE CROWNING OF HIS WORK

begettings these mirages; attend carefully to the savor of these fruits, seemingly so beautiful.

Let us not become attached to our garments any more than to the raiments of our intelligence, or to those of the body; they are but provisional instruments. Our will must seek refuge in the eternal. Let it abandon all the rest, for everything in us is due for renewal—each life's lights stands out from a shadow of death.

I repeat once more that Christic regenerations are not "perfectings," they are new births. Consider for a moment how our muscular strength increases through exercise, but only up to an insuperable limit—to pass beyond which, we must wait for our body to die and be reborn. So it goes also with our magnetic, mental, and passional forces. The healer, the thinker, and the artist can well multiply their esoteric trainings, disciplines, meditations, and aesthetic contemplations, but having once reached the maximum growth of the innate powers within each of them, they will go no further. Another hand, superior to theirs, will have to sow in their spirit another seed, a more vigorous one. This would be the time to examine, accuse, or blame the various practical systems of occultism, But a whole volume would not suffice to expound this cause, even summarily. Just recall the saying: "Unless the seed dies, it will bear no fruit."

In short, it is our duty and our right to utilize the forces that nature has entrusted us with.

Let us remember that to be sound, our labors must be directed towards God. If our intention remains thus constant, if our profound desires aim straight towards heaven, everything—labors, night-watches, worries, and illnesses—will reach the absolute and augment our eternal treasure.

This is how the soul of the disciple keeps in close contact

The Faithful Friend

with his Master in essential space. This is how, when their union, through ordeals endured steadfastly, becomes sufficiently intimate, the body or the bodies of the disciple, and the pure and radiant bodies of the omnipresent Word, come and go (simultaneously, so to say) through the thousand kingdoms of the world, fused by the flame of their reciprocal love.

This is the promise signified by the saying: "There where I am, there is my servant also." A state of soul is a "there," a site, a location in invisible space. From the four points of the globe, similar desires feel one another and unite; they always gather on their respective planes, but when they are sufficiently strong, they reunite even on the material plane.

The disciple is close to Jesus, then, because he harbors the same sentiments, because he burns from similar desires. His efforts result in fugitive reunions, in rapid colloquies—sometimes in the intellective, sometimes in the animic, occasionally in the magnetic fields. If the disciple has deployed an extraordinary ardor and an invincible perseverance, a physical contact takes place and the interplay of secondary causes combines in such a way as to have him spend a few years in the real, tangible, corporeal company of his Friend. We must reiterate the fact that this Friend goes much further afield than the disciple towards the meeting, because his love is infinite.

Man, actually, is capable only of a languid type of love; to fan the flame, the cold blasts of doubt, of despair, and of suffering are needed.

The Word hastens to meet the prodigal child, and the complaint: "Now my soul is troubled; Father save me from this hour," is the first stone that, rolling down the slope of the mystical mountain, wounds the divine feet.

THE CROWNING OF HIS WORK

What does Jesus call his soul? First, let us find what is taught orally in the synagogue, as this would be a natural expression for the Messiah to use.

According to the disciples of Moses, the universe unfolds from the will of the Ayn-Soph in four successive movements. The first movement is the emanation wrought by the divine persons and the divine names. The second movement is the creation, the extraposition, the abstract cosmic mind. The third is the formation, which means the divine economy, of the angelic hierarchies. The fourth is the "faction" or physical life. Finally, this latter is surrounded by a *caput mortuum*—matter, shells, or crust that does not have an existence per se.

Each of these five modes furnishes to the individual man a delegation of which the following is a short description: *yechidah*, the superessential unity and the inner divine presence being representative of Ayn-Soph; *chayah*, the outer glory to the composite and independent from it, so to speak; *neshamah*, the intellectual soul; *ruach*, the sensitive or irascible soul; *nephesh*, the central fire, the psyche, the vegetative, concupiscible soul; and finally, the body of matter (the physical body).

According to the Hebraic text, *nephesh* is the word Jesus uses in the verse we are studying; hence, it is the physical vitality within him it represents—the double that fears the approach of the terrible hours of the Passion, because he wanted to offer to all possible human sentiments the compassionate and mediating hospitality of his divine nature. We will find at each step of the final grand holocaust some new examples of that beneficence.

Time is a being. It is even the great coordinator of the masses. It is not time that assigns to each army corps its

The Faithful Friend

camp postings; time, rather, directs the soldiers according to the orders transmitted to them by the general. And, as each of the roles distributed to the creature causes it to produce one or other in germ, it has been written that "the knowledge of being forms the stages of time." The year, the month, the day, the hour, and so on are therefore like living tableaus in whose action we are forced to take part, and whose framework circumscribes the space necessary for our physical or psychic gestures. Even in reality, tableaus are not simple: their sense-perceptible appearance is formed by the interferences and refractions of various forms of time.

In their static state, creatures are at rest. In their dynamic state, the visits they make to one another are occasions for them to perform the work at hand, the means of their development, the school where they learn to know one another.

This is what might be said of the first part of the appeal launched by love throughout endless spaces. Barely has human frailty transpierced the soul of the Savior, than the divine force rises and shouts to the zenith of the universes the definitive triumph of faith: "Father, glorify your name!"

If every being radiates, if every creature, even the most miserable, possesses a splendor that must be discovered, whether it has been painfully acquired or generously given, there comes a moment in its existence when this splendor is totalized into a halo for the generality of men, and a glory for the elite. One finds the figurations of these radiances in the circles and the golden ovals surrounding the faces of certain Brahmanic gods, Buddhist sages, and Catholic saints. This is what the Kabbalah called the *Shekinah*.

On the other hand, a name is an algebraic formula. If the sense of touch is the door through which what is external reaches the nerves, so does the sense of taste reach the abdomen, the sense of smell reach the chest, and sight and hearing act as doors to the mental body. The eye perceives the fleeting, changing patterns of light; the ear perceives sounds, words, and names; and the mental body, when it acts without intermediaries, perceives thoughts and the normative numbers.

According to these data, the name of God is therefore the most synthetic formula through which the Absolute reveals itself to us. It happens that, when man has ventured too far on the road to perdition, the Absolute intervenes with greater tangible reality, either by means of an angelic message or by his Spirit abumbrating, overshadowing a chosen man, or by creating for itself a special physical organism.

The life of Christ is the archetype of this latter mode. This protagonist of the divine possesses total knowledge and perfect might. He is completely conscious of himself, of nature, and of God. But men, his poor sufferers, do not know him, or only very little: they will understand him only when, after long and painful crossings, they will have merited to be inscribed upon the Book of Life.

The mission of the king of angels remains quasi-imperceptible, almost irrational, since it comes from heaven itself—within and outside, above and beyond, the cosmic mass as it was taught a long time ago by the ancient Rishis, the Kings, and the Zohar. This quickening stirs nations down to their wombs, arouses the labyrinths of spirits, the magma of matter, without being sensed by anyone. In the shadow, it renovates minerals, plants, animals, and intelligences; it even brings in some unknown species. And one day this work of the king explodes—magnificent, universal, triumphant—before the dazzled eyes of creatures trembling from terror or ecstasy. Such is the "glory of the name."

The Faithful Friend

The ancient forerunner of this apotheosis was the secret judgment that more than two thousand years ago condemned the prince of this world, the lieutenant of Lucifer. Who is the being thus named? None of the ancient mythologies (no Chinese, Hindu, Persian pantheons), no system (not that of the gnostics or those of Pico de la Mirandola or of Agrippa) reveals an entity similar to that which the Christian Hermeticists and the Western mystics designate by that title. Let us, however, try to elucidate their theories.

The earth is composed, as any other creature, of a material envelope, a fluidic enormon ("vital principle") containing all the known and unknown physical forces, as well as an intelligent, conscious, and free self. The ponderable envelope is the *materia mundi*; the fluidic enormon or egg is the *spiritus mundi*—the astral part of the planet; the self is the *anima mundi*. Just as in man, the planetary self is solicited in two opposite directions, and so there are in him two centers: one of darkness, one of light.

In the universe, the chief or lord of the light is our Lord Jesus Christ. The lord of darkness is Lucifer. On earth, the former has a lieutenant, the lord of this world, through whom ascends all that is good as well as all the prayers said by the inhabitants of this globe; while the lieutenant of the second is the prince of this world, who centralizes all the evil committed here-below.

Before the coming of Christ, as a result of the millenary strayings of men, the prince of this world held supremacy over their intelligence and over the telluric forces. He and his army occupied the roads along which pass the various nutriments the cosmos sends us. He controlled the atoms, the mineral dusts, the vegetable seeds, the races, the fluids; all ideas, sciences, arts, as well as all rites, laws, spirits, and souls.

THE CROWNING OF HIS WORK

Through him and his henchmen all the emanations radiating from the earth would reascend: the departed, the messengers, the collectives, the invocations, idealistic desires, intellectual stresses, psychic sufferings, labors, ordeals of life, physiological fermentations, mute passivities, and alchemies of all kinds.

And he used his skillful tyranny stealthily to make the anguish of creatures serve his ends.

But the arrival of Christ wrenched away his scepter. The world passed from this deceptive tranquility to a battlefield; everything was overthrown; and the recoil, the backlash, of these inward seethings are recorded in the tumultuous history of the entire earth, and of Europe in particular. And the closer the race, the continent, and the planet come to the end, the more terrible the struggle will be.

Therefore, be "as wise as serpents": do not welcome or give your allegiance to anything without due consideration. Take care particularly to detect the kind of spirit that hides beneath the often sublime and fascinating allurements of polytheistic doctrines and hieroglyphic monuments. Remain vigilant until the Redemption has been completed, until such time as "the Savior, having risen, will have brought all men unto him."

Oneness, unity, is the beginning and the end of all things. Everything comes from the Father and returns to the Father; everything lives through the Son; everything vibrates through the Spirit. Being the model, the synthetic archetype, of all ideals, the Word necessarily attracts all human aspirations. The Word is the unique seed and the lost spark. But this seed functions inwardly with an intensive life, and this spark kindles the regenerative conflagration ablaze everywhere. It is the battle between heaven and hell.

The Faithful Friend

Our self, the product of our personal destiny, is saturated with the viruses of the prince of this world. We must dissociate those tenacious combinations to make new ones; and, as they are composed of the very substance of our fluidic, mental, and physical person, their dissolvant must be from a higher essence. Were the will independent from the composite it directs, it would suffice to fill that office; but because of the contamination of evil, it needs the accidental aid of grace, which it (the will) receives under the form of the influence of the Spirit, consciously or unconsciously, individually or collectively. Ecstasies and the diverse inner contacts described by contemplatives are, among the forms of spiritual aid, the most extraordinary yet the least efficacious.

The crowning of these immense labors foretells the coming of the reign of God. The Jews understood it to be a material kingship; the Far-Eastern people, under another name, conceived it as a mental state. Both of these opinions have some truth in them. The New Jerusalem will be both celestial and terrestrial. In its definitive state, it becomes the kingdom of God per se, amid the original and innate splendors of which the radiating beauties of beings, having finally emerged from dolor, shine with greater dazzling brilliance. But in the preparatory states, the New Jerusalem is realized, here and there, on all the planets whose task is perfected—even if only sometimes in the pure parts of these planets, of which it (the New Jerusalem) constitutes their beatific paradise: summarized images of the great divine harmony where all live and shine in pure love.

THE CROWNING OF HIS WORK

The Meeting of the Two Currents

A GUIDE ALWAYS ACCOMPANIES US. OCCASIONALLY, HE is a little ahead; but is it not so as to impel us to hasten? The errors and the enemies, which are the only ones able to delay us, disappear during the all too short periods of bliss wherein we enjoy the material presence of our Guide.

Apart from these moments, divine aid can reach us (through either our inferior or superior unconscious) only in the night, of which the motives of our acts are also born. This double domain, which diminishes in proportion to our degree of culture, is composed of the sediments left over from our previous lives—that is, through heredity, atavism, and the actual influence of our race, of our religion, of the planet, and of the solar system at the present time.

It is because it would be beyond our powers to direct ourselves, if we knew ourselves completely, that we receive internal and external counsels.

That is for the self. As for the non-self, we have visible and invisible enemies therein, the latter of which are far the more numerous. We do not have to encounter them until such time as we have become strong, so that, either in some state of sleep or when awake, psychic manifestations do not frighten us any more. In either case, help is always made available and at hand.

The genii referred to by Agrippa in his *Occult Philosophy* are not guides properly speaking; they are members of some particular spiritual tribe that periodically influences health, professions, the mental plane etc. They are the beings that govern astrological influences. Our true guides may be: a brother who has trodden the path ahead of us and retraces his steps for our benefit; an extraordinary "chosen" messen-

The Faithful Friend

ger especially commissioned because at that precise moment we find ourselves, unknowingly, to be the pivot of a grave enterprise; our guardian angel; or even a soldier of heaven with whom we saunter along for a while.

Our responsibility is that much greater because we are fully conscious of this guide. If ever you have contact with an envoy of heaven, do be careful. Much is expected from him to whom a great deal was given. Nothing from the invisible attains its full stature unless we give it a material form. The fact that we understand best the physical plane here-below indicates that our work *par excellence* must be to perform our topmost work on this particular plane.

Believe these things, even should you not comprehend them fully—intelligence sometimes needs to be jostled. We are not aware of the splendors within us—our ratiocinative imagination cannot even visualize it. This whole immense universe delegates representatives within our spirit. There is not a force, an idea, a flame; not a form, a demon, a genii, a god, whose ambassador we do not harbor! All the Olympian heavens dwell in the deeply-recessed regions of our selves; and in our secret center dwells the form of the Father: his Word, his Son.

The difficult thing is to evoke these mysterious presences in the cold circles of the intellect, in the smoky hotbeds of passion, in the sludge of the body. The air of these conscious regions is unbreathable for them, and their brilliance affronts the eyes of the mind.

Hence the labor of the sage is definitely to act according to what the old initiates taught—to purify the external vehicles so that they may become habitable to the internal gods. These are already Herculean tasks.

But the labor of the Christian is far more formidable.

THE CROWNING OF HIS WORK

It involves invoking the supernatural, the uncreated, the infinite. That is why you, disciples of the Son, who want to become "children of light"—your sufferings will be superhuman. Let not your courage weaken!

The sublime and candid Jacob Boehme rightly said that the world is magic. In this, at any event, he was in agreement, as we know, with the prehistorical Brahmans who schematized the universal process and the wheel-of-becoming in sacrifice. Every existence is an evolution; every evolution takes place through invocation of the objective superior and the evocation of the subjective superior by means of the corresponding inferiors (subordinates).

Enabling the cells of the material body, the inborn instruments of the conscious self, to become the instruments of the intuitive unconscious as well, changes their physical properties and chemical composition, and purifies their vital spirit as well. Thus, to evoke the superconscious powers that come from nature is to improve spiritual plants and transplant them to better soils.

But invoking the divine spark requires the plant to be uprooted, then transported to pure soil. Pure soil is not in the realm of the relative: this aura of the divine spark is the place of the Holy Spirit, the eternal Virgin within us. In this way, the faculties that have thus become supernatural will grow roots above and in the center in heaven, and flowers here-below as well as beyond this earth.

Thus, man as a whole, and everything that bears an eternal soul, possesses charity, knowledge, and faith in the innermost conscience. But only a small fraction of men enjoy a mental body pure enough for the supernatural seed of faith to germinate within. A still smaller fraction possess a few cells of the grey substance that the fideic vibration of

The Faithful Friend

the mental matter may reach—such as the religious writers do, for example. Among only a few, some cells of the etheric body vibrate in correspondence with this spark: these are the thaumaturgists who operate through prayers. And the two or three men in whom the cells of all the bodies (including their physical body) feel these radiations are those whom no ordeal intimidates: these are the true "soldiers."

Such a labor brings down a deiform fire and procures eternal recompense because the true characteristic of light is to rise. When light has terminated its course throughout the fields of matter, it returns to its principle enriched from the physical substances it has conquered, more brilliant because of the sufferings it endured; and it assumes (i.e., takes along with it) a part of the creature who was the theater of its mission.

Faith must emerge from its inner tabernacles. It has to force its way through the various envelopes that make up our earthly personality, our mask: the more subtle these are, the more readily it accepts that one. So it is easier to believe intellectually, philosophically: faith of the heart is less common; faith of physical mentality, of everyday life, is rare; but the faith that reaches down into vitality is unfathomable, undecipherable—this is the kind of faith Jesus says can move mountains.

You can establish the same scale for each of the other moral virtues, and for the other personalities that hinge upon a similar soul.

All atoms, material, etheric, intellectual, etc., that have received and assimilated a ray of this central faith are uprooted from the natural earth and replanted in this land of the living, which some mystics call the Celestial Virgin.

THE CROWNING OF HIS WORK

Understand that the divine virtues are forces; agility is a physical virtue; faith is a spiritual force—and because faith is the base, the stem, the driving center of the act that we speak of it first.

The act is born from the will. The will becomes good or evil according to its inner motivation, its intent. Therefore, the purest, the simplest, and the loftiest intention unfolds or is acquired through faith.

This work of acclimatization is common to all creatures. However, only men possess the wisdom of the *spiritus mundi*, and beings inferior to man do this work on the plane of nature by calling upon gods. The Christian does it on the supernatural plane.

To help inferior realms, such as minerals, plants, and animals, we must not deplete them for our own benefit, as we tend to do with intensive farming. We must not obscure their instincts by bad example, because the stone you throw at an adversary smacks of your fury. We must never thwart their evolution, because mistreatment of a horse embitters its spirit. In principle, we are the kings of nature; we are the only ones who carry the seeds of divine virtues. All of the other lights of our spirit, of our intellect, our courage, our etheric fluids, of our body; all the other energies of the stone, of the plant, the animal, the star, the demon, or the elemental spirit, are but the changeable and multiple interplays of the three pure divine lights moving upon the substantial veils of created forms.

The domain of faith is the religious sphere. But from there, faith radiates upon the hypotheses of the philosopher, the enthusiasms of the artist, the enterprises of the leader of a country, with more or less luster according to whether the man is deeply religious or not.

The Faithful Friend

However, throughout all worlds, lightning flashes most brilliantly upon the darkest skies. Thus Jesus disappears to offer mankind the occasion to expend a more intensive energy in their search for him. Were everything given to everyone in a lump, no one would work anymore—for in our best impulses selfishness still lies dormant.

God has put us on earth for our advantage and not for his. By acquiring and increasing our merits we develop virtues. The philosophical, esoteric, or religious systems that tend to keep man away from action kill the life within him and around him—it is the work of the perverted one, the Antichrist.

If we do not have faith, the next best thing is to work without expecting to receive any personal benefit therefrom. When we have faith, we work for God. Thus, not having tied our acts to ourselves, neither will they bind us to themselves. By offering our efforts to him from whom we derive our strength, we will exalt their scope up to the Almighty—beyond all form—to the eternal.

There are in fact two steps in the processes by which the self unites with its milieu: first, it perceives the other "selves" out of which this milieu is composed, then it assimilates their substance, it absorbs them.

Perception presupposes a sensation. For a sensation to be felt, there has to be an object, a subject, and a transmitting organ. The eye being the most perfect organ we have (as embryology and philosophical anatomy demonstrate), the gospel always uses it as the model of perception. That is why the gospel always refers to those who could not believe, or who did not want to believe, as "blind": "could not," because the organ of sight was lacking; "did not want to," because they were willfully preventing it from functioning.

THE CROWNING OF HIS WORK

On the other hand, having once perceived an object, we assimilate it, we feed upon it—in the physical, the etheric, the intellectual, and in the spiritual planes, according to the category to which it belongs. The more subtle is the organ for a rapid assimilation to take place, the faster we evolve. Because matter, from terrestrial granite up to sparkling points of the empyrean, is never anything but the instrument of force, the field of the Spirit's experiments.

So, the closer to nothingness the individual stands, the more immutable, inalterable, insensitive, callous, indifferent, frozen, and hard he is. The closer he is to life, the more mobile, multifarious, ardent, compassionate, sensitive, and open he is. Nature shows this in the scale of types, from spiritual to material, from adamantine to attenuated.

Scripture calls those who cannot understand divine things "hardened" and those who cannot receive the light "hard-hearted" because we feed only on what is analogous to us; and our essential organ, which characterizes us, is the temple of God, whose location is reserved in our heart.

When we believe, without daring to admit it, because of what people might say, it is because the compartments of our spirit are already occupied by worries about respectability, tranquility, social position; faith then withers, and we need to make up for it with stimulants. Thus the Israelites, who feared the synagogue when they came back a few hundred years later, were consumed with the intense desire of making the Deliverer known to all people—they became missionaries and the martyrdom they endured brought to their faith the necessary strength to make up for time lost.

Let us express our convictions without fanaticism, without prejudice, without arrogance, hate, or fear. The more we suffer for our beliefs, the greater the number of little

The Faithful Friend

beings dying within us to that end; so do our convictions increase and advance towards triumph.

We must live and express our ideal through our conduct, our thoughts, and our sentiments. Little by little, the very form of our body, our attitudes and gestures, will be modeled upon it; and little by little, we will incarnate that ideal, and its angel will dwell within us.

It is only in appearance that we choose our ideal. Rather, this ideal chose us, or was sent to us because we offered it the terrain and facilities most favorable for its development—or, maybe, for other reasons. If we try to escape this ideal, then, instead of being nurtured and growing, it withers. And, as true justice wants it to survive, there comes a time when the lazy man must suffer a great deal and cover much ground in a short time. The higher and purer this ideal, the more imperious becomes the duty of incarnating it, and the heavier the penalty for our indolence. Thus it is that some choose martyrdom while others err towards suicide.

However, we are never accounted reprehensible for first getting a clear idea of the state of things before undertaking some task. We must, moreover, closely examine our tendencies, especially those that seem loftiest: if they conform to what we know of the law, we must realize them; if not, we must forget them.

Let us emphasize yet again that everything is alive: from this sheet of paper upon which I write, down to the illness that may lie in wait behind the door, everything moves in its own sphere, just as physical bodies, dreams, and cerebral abstractions do. Everything must be dealt with as such; and all licit means are excellent for procuring the nourishment that our ideal deserves and has a right to receive.

THE CROWNING OF HIS WORK

Never employ ruse, lies, or violence. Never defend an idea with weapons contrary to its nature.

This Meeting is a Being

THE INTRINSIC, ESSENTIAL BELIEF OF CHRISTIANITY IS the identity of the Divine Persons. The old liturgical hymns, those that only Benedictine monks know, occasionally state this mysterious and harmonious antinomy with grandiose power.

In the operation of the Absolute, its realization is synchronous with conception; and the Relative as a whole, according to the indefinite variations of its innumerable planes, reflects the parity between the first impulse (the Word) with the primary motive power (the Father) by means of the first driving power (the Holy Spirit).

This is the foundation of the ancient magic science of correspondences, mother of the science of signatures.

When contemplated in this manner, from without, cosmic life is so complex that it defies analysis, whereas, when viewed from within, it is one. It follows that esotericists abandon the analysis of positive sciences only to rejoin a plane that may seem synthetic with respect to the former; but is still nothing but analysis from another point of view. It is so, because the conception we form of the world is always correspondent to our own inner state. Are we scatter-brained? If so, our knowledge and understandings are sparse, far-flung, dispersed; were we able to become one (a unity) from the bottom of our heart to our finger tips, our science would be one and our power one.

The perceptions we were just referring to come from two deep sources: instinct from below, intuition from above.

The Faithful Friend

The first intuitive inkling man has of God is through faith; his first perception thereof is inner illumination; his first assimilation thereof is the new birth. The Messiah is the artisan of these three works. He is the crown of creation because he alone has maintained with his Father that unity which all other beings have cloven asunder. He is the column, the pillar, that supports the world, as the Zohar puts it. He is the solemn moment, present everywhere simultaneously, where those who have strayed return to their center. This is what he came for, to lead those who have strayed out of darkness. He is the "fleuron," the finial upon whom all the lines of the temple converge. He is the living answer to the agonizing shriek of dolor and of hope of the ancient generations. He is the light through whom everything is alive—even darkness, evil, ignorance, and death. He is the realization of all our yearnings of faith. He is the reality of all our ideals, the physician for all physical, social, intellectual, moral, scientific, or philosophical ills. He is all these things because there does not exist any situation, any state of soul or misery, for which our Jesus is not the total remedy. Within himself, voluntarily and organically, he is a naught, in order that in him everything proceeds from the Father.

As an example, let us examine ourselves. Each of us has a different "ego," a different self; our physical body is individualized, separate, because there is in that body a notion of the "I," without which we would be but an amorphous parcel of the whole. And of course this same reasoning applies to each and every other "ego." Hence, if the central self, the heart, the will, becomes a naught, an exaltation beyond nature takes place, and then an identification with the absolute.

THE CROWNING OF HIS WORK

This is how Christ considers himself as a naught, and why he is the veritable child of God, the Son, from the apex to the bottom of his total being. He heals, he suffers, he judges, he speaks, as soon as the Father wants him to do those things—and only then. That is why he represents the prototype, the perfect model, of the savior, of the physician, and of the guide.

As none of the forces he projects belongs to him personally, they become, in this relative world, the forms of the will of the Father. This is why his acts, not being from him, but from the Father, possess a life of their own, a free spontaneity, thanks to which they remain fecund and immortal: they are angels, messengers of the Father, who pass through the being of Christ in order to acquire certain powers.

In fact, these sparks of pure light cannot be absorbed by us directly. They are too dazzling, too powerful, too strange for our different organisms not to be frightened by their presence. It is necessary that they first go through some adjustment. But their intermediary must be vast enough, sensitive enough, powerful and wise enough, so that nothing our immense nature contains may remain foreign to it. Now, since this intermediary must embody all worldwide essences and all creatural types, it can only be the Word himself in his cosmic aspect.

That is how these very pure, innocent angels, strangers to this lower world (who are the essence itself of the words and acts of Jesus and whom we would not understand were they to reveal themselves openly to us) assume or array themselves when they pass through the All-Compassionate with something tender and familiar that enthralls us.

In fact, whatever is possible for us to perceive of the perpetual activity of Christ, of its constancy and of its magni-

The Faithful Friend

tude, shows just how complex it is: Christ is *one*, the redemptive gesture of the Son of God is *unique*, and its force always remains *equal*, identical to itself. But in the relative state, salvation is offered to *all* creatures, according to the *infinite* nuances of their individual receptivities, and the initial eternal unity of the mercy of the Father dissociates itself *innumerably* in the temporal.

Each of these fragmentary beams is an angel according to the meaning proper to Christian theology. The angels of the other religions are spirits, elemental spirits, or composite gods in whom the good and the bad, the true and the false, strength and weakness, interblend in variable proportions. Only the angels in service to Christ are pure spirits, entities independent of space and time, intelligent and powerful wills. Those wills are the very wills of the Father, for otherwise the angel would fall from the rank of pure spirit to that of a creature similar to us, a natural creature. The angel sees God constantly, sees two objects only: God and the goal whereto God sends him. The army of angels, the angelical universe, has God as its center. It is the kingdom of heaven about which Jesus so often speaks. It penetrates all other worlds, saturating them. It is, as Jesus states, within us, because nothing is refractory to its radiance or opaque to its splendor.

In short, the kingdom is developing indefinitely, because it is life *par excellence*, because each activity of the Father is an angel, and because that the Father acts without cease.

The solicitude of the Father is therefore a veritable supernatural world amid the thousands of natural worlds: a world with its stars, its oceans, its earths, and its creatures; a world widespread throughout creation and penetrating the whole of it, from its densest planes up to its most subtle ethers; a world of pure spirit whose inhabitants live in obedience and with fervor; a world where all is light without shadow and movement without obstacle; and finally, a world whose population increases through each of our prayers and each of our sorrows because each of them elicits at all times a response from the Father, even when we do not hear it.

Focus the eyes of your heart upon this spectacle. See Jesus keeping close watch over all beings as each expression of the feelings that pass through his immeasurable heart becomes an angel soaring towards the object of his solicitude. Heed Jesus listening to all appeals, complaints, and supplications as each word of his responses becomes a pacifying angel, a consoling angel, a therapeutic angel. Each movement of his magnificent being, each gesture, each wink, creates an angel. And we who strive to become his disciples, the closer we come to him, the more numerous becomes the cohort of intermediary angels who link us to his glory, the more rapid becomes their zeal, and the more powerful their obedience.

But do not be mistaken. You will draw angels to you only if you serve Jesus solely, and if you invoke Jesus solely. If by default of faith your heart stops one second to invoke an intermediary between Jesus and yourself, the angels will flee, and mixed, composite beings will replace them. You will be stepping out into the external. This is so, because the angel essentially is an act of God; and for God to act, one must see nothing but him and address him only. The greater depth you attain to reach God, the more beautiful, stronger, purer will the angel of his response be. For that, you must forget that there are elementary spirts and gods, forget that there are saints, even forget that there are angels.

The Faithful Friend

Each time you starve selfishness, you nourish one of these angels. As you do not know the road through which the Shepherd wants to lead you, practice all modes of spiritual abstinence whenever occasion presents itself. Thus will you gain a foothold in the world of grace. You will become a member of it. You will give your questioners the right answers without having had recourse to any means of information. A sick person about whom someone speaks to you will be healed without your knowing how. You will bring comfort to a destitute person with a few words that to you seem dull and inadequate. In short, you will progress towards the annihilation of self that mystical books speak of, that you thought you had already attained when you first set out upon the gospel path. You now know that this path is very long. Do not be discouraged. You will reach the end.

But no quietism! Bestir yourselves briskly until you fall exhausted from fatigue for the sake of good works. It is only at this price that you will receive that sense of the divine by which your heart orients itself towards the one and only Jesus. What you have just read has no other purpose than to furnish you the occasion to be stripped, to reach a state of denudation far more severe than the ones you had experienced so far.

⊕

Christ is the rendezvous of all antinomies; he is freedom personified and the complete slave; the omniscient, the all-powerful who proclaims he knows nothing and is unable to do anything but what his Father allows him: their reciprocal love, which is the Spirit, identifies one with the other. Because of the gravity of these conceptions, this is all that prudence and respect permit me to say.

THE CROWNING OF HIS WORK

What the Father orders is real, true, and living. And all this is the Son. His every word and deed is therefore a form of eternal life. In us, the faculty of expression (which is a supraphysical begetting) is fragmented, dismembered, in the form of the body, of the gesture, the attitude, the voice, the mimicry, the glance, and the work. In God, the faculty of expression is one. In us, it is agonizing; in God, it is immortal; in us, it is puny; in God, it is victorious.

On the whole, the Word Jesus, from the instant of his true birth at the dawn of creation to the glory of his total culminating splendor at the crepuscule of the world, will have ceaselessly obeyed without a second's interruption, without having relaxed his embrace of the Father, without ever having averted his regard. From all this result the characteristics of simplicity of the definitive and of the absolute found in his words. And their powerful influence is still felt today—down to the shape, the forms, of stones, of plants, and of all things—in spite of the disorders men and devils have multiplied in this world.

Renunciation

PRACTICED ACCORDING TO THE PROFOUND AND VAST plenitude that is the ground proper to gospel counsels, renunciation is equivalent to a death. When Jesus reminds us that unless a seed dies it will not reproduce, he wants, among other allusions, to remind us that in the fields of our person, the Father in the beginning sowed and still sows a great many species of seeds, and that similarly to those in our farmlands they must be submitted to a physical death in order to be reborn to the life of the Spirit, increased a hundredfold in number and virtues. Doubtless, ascetics

The Faithful Friend

who insist on repeating in various ways that we must kill selfishness state the essential, and this precept would suffice were we to track down the innumerable shoots of this venomous root with the constancy, energy, and care necessary. But we are so inattentive, our life is so often in a state of drowsiness, and our thought merely a reverie, that we need the most pressing exhortations, unflagging repetitions, to persuade us to undertake and shoulder the mystical effort.

Selfishness is our self as a whole; it is the permanent kernel of the self, around which aggregate like corals the sediments brought without respite by the milieus of all kinds in which it sojourns from the time it sallied out of heaven up to its re-entry into the House of the Father. If it is true that we have lived upon other worlds before arriving upon this one, we can imagine from the mass of contributions we receive from this earth, of what enormous cosmic deposits our personality is constituted. We carry the physiological, mental, and moral heritage of all of our ancestors without exception; we carry the immaterial sediments of past centuries, of the countries, religions, social classes, and diverse cultures; the customs, the principles and examples, in short the sum-total of work that the whole of humanity precipitates within us from the billions of impalpable yet active molecules that make us what we are. That was the past: destiny. They are the data of the problem of our present lifetime. From this inscrutable base emerges the architecture of our character, the mental *a priori* that we never sift through the sieve of criticism, the conventions that seem to us unquestionable, the lies that have finally taken on the figures of truth, the vices that we believe to be virtues. How suspicious and distrustful should we be of ourselves! No one is really vigilant, because no one dares annihilate his self.

THE CROWNING OF HIS WORK

Let us learn how to judge ourselves with the same lucid rigor with which we judge our brother. Are not all of our slanders summarized into one? Do not the motes we perceive in the eyes of our companions reveal the beam deeply sunken within our own eyes? Is there not a common taint in the conscience of everyone and a sole vice in the manner with which we judge one another? Because in all of us our real vices are the very ones we are not conscious of anymore we do not sense our profound corruptions anymore; and in the form of the perversity peculiar to each of us, we end up by believing it to be a virtue. The old miser believes his miserliness to be a strength, the ambitious man has persuaded himself he serves his people, and the dyed-in-the-wool envious man cuts a figure of innocent victim. When one recognizes one's sins, it means that evil has not yet taken root, that it is still at a certain distance from our conscience: evil and conscience are still two. But when we stop realizing that we are acting wrongly, if when evil-doing we think we are doing good—this means that evil has become an integral part of our personality.

Thus each of our effective steps forward towards good entails the death of the correspondent evil in us, which was ourselves. And these moral agonies, which are the most useful and most fecund among agonies, are on par with the parallel strippings or abnegations in the physical or intellectual realms.

In fact, where sentiment, sensation, ideas, and volition are concerned, or where pleasure or pain, sympathy or antipathy, reality or illusion are concerned, as soon as we become aware of one of these facts it is because this fact or sensation is external to the self: it is an allotment, a contribution, a nutriment that is going to be assimilated more or

The Faithful Friend

less. As soon as one of these nutriments has embedded into the "us" (the "us" body, the "us" soul, the "us" spirit, the "us" will), the conscience dims away and even tends to disappear from them. These nutriments rejoin the enormous ancient warehouse of similar nutriments provided long ago by all the environs surrounding us: physico-chemical cells; sparks of the social, national, ethnic, intellectual, artistic, or religious life; emanations of the fluidic or etheric currents wherein our immaterial organs bathe; legacies from our ancestors and of past centuries; radiations from the superior worlds as well as miasmas from the inferior ones. From these profound strata spring our profound forces: instincts, inborn ideas, *a priori* opinions, spontaneous desires. So if we want to become free and ripe for the eternal birth, we must also break away definitely from these profound dynamisms.

The methodical scrutiny of our conscience aims straight at these subterranean denudations. Studying our dreams and visions helps in this inquiry, on condition of pursuing it more deeply than what manuals furnish. The psychological conscience in fact usually records only the refracted images of the veritable scene experienced by our immortal spirit during dreams. Upon awakening, our memory, no matter how precise, relates but the shadows shown upon the mental screen. Of course these shadows suffice as presages, as warnings, as encouragements, as lessons; but they do not suffice anymore when we want to analyze the central self and separate the adventitious from it. In that sense, Freud's psychoanalysis may be of use if one extricates it from the morbid allurement that brought it fame. Even the most absurd dream contains or hides an exact notion. However, there exists no general method for this particular research.

THE CROWNING OF HIS WORK

Each sleeper has his own equation, and the psychological problems simple to a superficial observer become extremely complicated in proportion to the depth of their analysis, only to become simple again, much later, only when one has reached the state to accost them from the within.

Moreover, all the impressions we have during waking hours, as well as those we have during sleep, may serve as points of departure for the study of one's self. But we must make distinctions between the studies that serve to know one's self theoretically from those that serve to live more fully. The disciplines given in esoteric schools to develop astral faculties and metaphysical powers are to the real knowledge of the self what the work in the operating amphitheater is to the medical art. To become fully conscious of all that happens, to become fully conscious of this very consciousness, and to be able to maintain this state—in short, using Christ's expression, "to be on watch"—is the course one must follow to realize that we are ignorant of life. And from this almost imperceptible but basic ignorance, situated at the origin of man's reasoning, bursts forth, when the psychic organism can support it, the illumination towards which all contemplatives are aiming.

But let me repeat: this illumination remains individualistic, incommunicable, and untransmissible.

Ardent searchers possessing a vigorous intellect and an imperious will-power strive to acquire it by the apparently most direct means: abstraction and concentration. Thus were the scholarly methods of India, China, Alexandria, and Persia conceived. Closer to us, so did the Comte de Lautréamont, Nietzsche, Max Stirner, and Lev Schestov work. But the other searchers, to whom the Father judges it timely to reveal his Son, take another path: instead of with-

The Faithful Friend

drawing, they exteriorize; instead of abstracting they go into life, cultivate life; instead of isolating themselves, they go out into the world, mixing with the crowd. Thereby, instead of attaining an inner, artificial, metaphysical, geometrical, mathematical, and immobile unity, they attain the living, real, and mobile unity organized by the pure Spirit. It is the triple communion with the Word through thought, love, and act that alone determines this transubstantiation of the self.

As you clearly can see, the fault of these non-Christic methods is to direct the effort solely on *one* of our centers: on the physiological center for the occultists; on the intellectual center for the philosophers; on the aesthetic center for the artists; on the volitive center for the highest adepts. In contrast, the Christian, whose sole motive is love, gathers his multiple faculties towards a constant collaboration by soliciting them, meanwhile permitting them to take full initiative. Instead of inflecting his faculties forcefully into the ramifications of some inner asceticism, he imparts to them a central direction: charity. He tells them: "Love first and always, and then do whatever you want."[4] It follows that spiritual growth develops with care and harmony: the center of gravity is never lost since it is fixed upon the Word, whose moves it follows through that fervent, faithful imitation of which love is the principle. The inevitable reactions of darkness, interior as well as exterior, are brought to a minimum. Thus the disciple sweeps along, in his ascension, the greatest possible number of his brothers, besides a great many other creatures, because life alone knows how to communicate with and stir life.

[4] A paraphrase of St Augustine.

THE CROWNING OF HIS WORK

Fasts, renunciations, and deaths are the three stages of the inner cataclysm that precedes the new birth that Jesus explains to Nicodemus. The moment this eternal dawn rises within us, the walls of destiny crumble down, the centuries-old sediments that were crushing us fall, and our whole resuscitating being thirstily absorbs the blessed life and yearns for eternal light and liberty. We become angels again, but "very wise" angels as the poet said, omniscient angels, because from now on nature cannot hide anything from us. We again become resplendent unities who love, think, and will by means of the same pure act: the Father adopts us once and for all, and Christ calls us his younger brothers.

In bold strokes, this is our future. Doubtless, this sketch remains imprecise. But no matter how strongly I try to accentuate it, the scene is so rich, the personages so numerous, their faces so distant, that the finest painter would despair delineating that which is inexpressible. It is up to you to fill in the vacant spaces of the canvas, up to your fervors to transport you to the summits. Whatever I may ever tell you will not be anything but making allusions to the arcana of the light. May they augment your mystical hunger and thirst *ad infinitum*. May you never appease either one except through a perfect communion with the sacrifices and sufferings of our Lord Jesus.

Palm Sunday

RELIGIOUS WRITERS HAVE MOST TOUCHINGLY TOLD IN detail the story of the triumphal entry of Jesus into Jerusalem so close to his Passion, referring to his humble mount, the palms of joyful greeting, and the enthusiastic acclaim

The Faithful Friend

from the populace. But they have failed to explain the veritable reason behind this manifestation.

In nature, everything goes in pairs, whether in oppositions or concordances. And particularly in this great epic of the Good News, the action's march is dual. On the one side, the cortège of heaven is coming down: the Precursor in front; then the Messiah surrounded by his double following of chosen disciples and serving angels; finally the army of men and the cohorts of the spirits of nature. On the other side, going up, is the cortège from the earth: the priests surround Herod, the Sadducees and Pharisees hasten, guided by the invisible agents of Mammon, Molock, and Satan, followed by the vast masses of polytheism, enchained by the rites riveted to the simulacra of the genii and of the gods of the *spiritus mundi*. The two cortèges come to meet at the crest of Mt Moriah, the site of the first skull,[5] at the foot of the universal Tree of the Cross.

For the past four thousand years, ever since the Nephilim and the Gibborim of the Sepher, the leaders would triumph from their chariots and from the top of the monumental terraces; for the past four thousand years, the people were acclaiming them under rods and chains; for the past four thousand years the kings presented themselves in the name of the false lord, were lauded aloud but accursed *sotto voce*; and these days of triumph were days of rejoicing only in the squalid dens of the cities and in men's sordid hearts.

For these enthusiastic cheers to become sincere, for the benedictions to take wing towards a goal totally worthy of the original nobility of the human heart, there had to come a given moment when the acclamations would reach the

---

[5] Golgotha or Calvary (both words meaning "skull").

THE CROWNING OF HIS WORK

King of Kings. The time had come for Jesus, after having endured all the variations of humiliations and tortures, to show us how to behave when triumph comes, how to await it instead of seeking it, how to accept it, and finally, how to bring it to conclusion.

The enthusiasm on the part of the people of Jerusalem is spontaneous. Jesus knows it is his due, and he explains how nature and men are not totally perverted, since the crowds' acclamations spring of their own accord, and since "if the disciples had not spoken, the stones would have cried out." Finally, he crowns this manifestation with the prophetic tears he sheds upon the nefarious future of this obstinate city that wants neither to know him nor to recognize him after the expulsion from the temple of the merchants, profaners, and thieves, nor on the day following his cursing the sterile fig-tree.

Taking these facts into consideration, it will not be difficult to extract from them the notions of cosmology, of alchemy, of lofty psychology that they slightly veil. But to begin with, the strange episode of the fig-tree, which seems so discordant with the characteristic humility of the Savior, requires an explanation.

I will only concern myself with the actual fact: a tree cursed because it did not bear fruit out of season.

A tree, as well as any other creature, possesses a share of intelligence and liberty; Jesus is the master of nature. The two axioms that the witnesses of the miracle admitted to *a priori*, we—you and I—will also admit, since otherwise there would be no reason for me to tell you or for you to listen to me.

As far as it is possible to understand the motives of the Savior, he cursed the fig-tree for three reasons, without

The Faithful Friend

being angry at all, anymore than he was a while back when chasing the vendors from the temple.

The fig-tree should not have resisted Jesus's demand and should have presented him with fruits. A man who refuses to obey an explicit order from heaven, who does not at least attempt to satisfy it, shoulders the same responsibility as this tree; and unless mercy comes to his rescue, he risks the same fate. Nothing subsists except through the vibrations of the Word of God. If anyone resists him, he is done for; he suffers the same fate as the non-conductor body, which, resisting the passage of the current, is volatized if the current is strong enough.

Let us glance at the second motive. Upon the surface of our globe, climactic distributions as well as all other manifestations of earthly life change, from heat on up to civilization. Today, Palestine is truly a desert if one compares it to the luxuriant orchard it was two thousand years ago. Remember that any general phenomenon begins with an isolated phenomenon. The death of the Bethany fig-tree marked the beginning of this sterilization, because the soil that had proven inhospitable to divine life caused natural life to withdraw from it.

Lastly, by proffering this entreaty, Christ gave mankind of the future proof of his humility. In fact, to fell a tree is to kill a being.

This evil is inevitable and doubtless necessary when the act is not a caprice. The obligation in which we find ourselves forced to perform it is part of the spiritual accounting where oftentimes we cancel a debt by contracting a new one in order to save time. Such evil will be greater or lesser according to the more or less selfish use we will make of that tree. By eliminating a vegetable existence, Jesus also lessened our responsibility in a similar case. He has given us a precedent for mercy. The accountants of nature will be a little less severe towards the delinquents if the Master of them all was guilty of the same offence.

As to the purification of the temple, when we broaden the frame of this episode to the limits of creation, we are led to expand our ideas beyond the temple and the merchants. The universe is the temple of God. All parts of the universe, even the collective, moral, and intellectual entities, are temples as well. As long as the gods, the forces of nature, mathematical and just laws, prevail therein, commerce will be engaged in. Beings barter among themselves things of a lesser value for things of the greatest value possible.

When the Word enters into one of these temples in the center of which the essential flame of the self burns, his logical gesture is to drive the vendors out. God never barters, never makes an exchange, he only makes a gift. Whether it concerns a sun, a science, a race, an illness—the contract the Father seems to offer is always a deal of dupes, a one-sided bargain. The law of the world is justice; the law of hell is violence and lies; but the law of heaven is benevolence.

When the reign of God will be established on earth, there won't be any more commerce, not even for material necessities. True "communism" will reign.

The Rite of Union

JOHN IS THE ONLY EVANGELIST WHO SPEAKS OF THE washing of the feet. Before relating this episode, he explains the profound reasons for this ceremony: "Jesus knew well that the Father had left everything into his hands, knew that he came from the Father and that he was going back to

The Faithful Friend

the Father." (John 13:3–4) It being a fact that the Messiah is the Lord of all creatures and of creation, he can do whatever he wants. As he was to leave the earth shortly, he had to leave them memories, witnesses, and continuators of his work. But the apostles would not have been capable of fulfilling this task had they not been completely extricated from the laziness and fears inherent to instinctive matter, the physiological localization of which is in the feet.

Good intentions are not sufficient, they have to be followed by an act. Man, who grows corrupt from inner to outer—from heart to intelligence, mentality, etheric fluids, and various bodies—starts repenting from the outer to the inner. But the *work* of repentance and of conversion begins in the heart. It takes time to purify intelligence, etheric fluids, physical cells. As long as there are still some of these cells vitiated by evil, the work of the "soldier" remains uncertain and precarious. This physical purification is the most painful, long-lasting, and furthest outside our power, because of the tightly-woven relationships between matter and evil. This is one of the secret reasons for the action of Christ washing the feet of his disciples. He was at the same time purifying their physical vitality as a whole.

Besides which, he was teaching them, insofar as they are men, how the superior must be the servant of the inferior. He emphasizes this voluntary humiliation by taking off his cloak: by disrobing. Then, to stress its inner meaning, he reveals himself such as he is, by underscoring the condition of the supreme beatitude, which is to help and assist our brothers, even the subalterns in all conceivable modes.

Here one could find sufficient subject matter for esoteric applications. For that, one could study the meanings of and the correspondences between bread, water, clothing, feet, and heels. One could discover certain rapports between this act and Adam's sin (of which it is the counterpart). But these are distant, abstract things that for us ordinary men have no immediate expediency.

Visualize this simple scene taking place within the whitewashed walls of some cool dark room, while outside the flamboyant sun is bursting upon the canvas of an ultramarine sky above the variegated clothing of the natives. Jesus is seated at the center of a long table at the place of honor. His host has the second place, on his right. John is on his left, the side of the heart. Then comes Peter, the priest, who addresses himself to the mystic to find out something. Then comes Judas, the treasurer who will become the criminal. The whole ulterior history of the future Church is here, as the contemplatives have never ceased to say.

In the primitive Church up to the time of Constantine, Easter was a mystery set apart. On that day a collection was taken up, which would later be replaced by gifts, donations, and honorariums to the priests. St Hildegarde vituperated about the abuses of this custom. On the other hand, the very fine practice of having this ceremony preceded by a public and general reconciliation began.

The blessing of the oils took place the same day.

Easter represents the passage of our present life, which the seventy years of exile to Babylon prefigured, to eternal life, and to the heavenly Jerusalem (St Augustine's *Enerratio* in Psalm 118). Invisibly, Easter reunites the individual to the Christian collectivity (Guillaume de Paris) because, according to the Bishop of Hippo (St Augustine), the body and blood of Christ are the Christendom of which he is both the soul and bridegroom, just as the human spirit is the master and the groom of the body.

The Faithful Friend

This rite is found not only with Melchizedek, high-priest according to the social order, but also (if one goes back far enough in centuries past) in the ancient Theban and Hindu sanctuaries. The wheat and the vine, as widespread as they are, are two mysterious plants to the beings to whom the Father conferred something special when they appeared here on earth. Their stem, their structure, their sign (one might say, the shape of their leaves and fruit), bear, for whoever knows how to read, the signature or the imprint of their spiritual virtues. Here we find another new example of heaven's activity—heaven abundantly multiplies the creatures it has particularly blessed, while nature has great difficulty to perfect a minimal elite of its productions.

Peasants are right when they respect bread and wine. Do not waste bread, the most necessary item to life. Should you find a piece of bread on the street, pick it up and put it aside, that it may still be utilized. It was made primarily for men, a little for some animals; but it must not be thrown into a garbage can.

The most comprehensible symbolism of the Last Supper is reconciliation. And even when, venturing into intellectual regions inappropriate to our needs here, one seeks in the natural history of fluids, in magic, in metapsychism, in ecstatic mysticism, for other meanings of this ceremony, one will never find anything but this same idea—reconciliation—specified, broadened, extended, or sublimated.

Before having realized what is commonplace (which means before having been willing to invite our bitterest enemies to our table), please note and understand that it is useless to look for these mysteries. What you would find would be imaginary. Besides, Jesus never fails to warn us in his prudent fashion. He does not forbid scientific research.

THE CROWNING OF HIS WORK

He merely contents himself repeating the one commandment: "Love ye one another"—in other words, do unto our brothers what he has done for us all.

Following this, how can we explain Peter's denial and the apostles fleeing? If they were pure, how could they have succumbed to fear? This disconcerting act of cowardliness took place for three reasons.

Primarily, Jesus wanted to suffer alone because he always chose the most difficult alternatives. He had to experience simultaneously the worst physical pains and the inexpressible discouragements of future foreseeable treacheries, plus the dagger-stabbings of sudden abandonments. Never will we be sufficiently convinced that the Messiah assumed all possible kinds of suffering, not for ascetic reasons but as the obligatory consequence of the works he had undertaken.

Neither do we comprehend the horror which saturated that day of his Passion. The most tragic and frightful hours adventurers recall having endured are but pale clouds compared to the terror that came crashing down upon this spot on earth that day. The seers do not exaggerate when they state that hell was fully unleashed. Not one man in the place of Christ could have suffered for a quarter of an hour the unutterable pangs of these hidden tortures.

Also, was it not necessary that all the dastardly, base actions of succeeding generations receive a mystical exculpation in advance? If men such as the apostles, after having had so many favors bestowed upon them, proved to be pusillanimous, the angels at the next judgment will not be able to treat too rigorously all of the thousands of weak, lukewarm, and indolent men who, for the past two thousand years have been betraying heaven's cause.

The Faithful Friend

Perenniality of Union

THE MYSTERIES WE ARE NOW CONCERNED WITH ARE all related to supernatural phenomena. We are not expected to understand them as one does a mathematical theorem, but to feel them as one appreciates a work of art or savors the scent of a saintly soul.

As for natural phenomena, we have a ponderable physical body that moves in a three-dimensional space. It possesses a double that functions in another space, as indicated in telepathic phenomena. So also do we have a mental body constructed out of a particular substance together with organs, centers, plexuses, and canals through which we perceive and that also moves in a particular space of which we are made aware during our meditative activities. At this stage ends the plane of the conscience.

Beyond this plane begins the domain of intuition, of the heart, of our veritable life. And this center, free from all conditions, from any form of space or time, radiates throughout our whole being down to its physical state. Thus a hair, a neuron, the smallest molecule of hemoglobin, the least muscle fiber, possesses a cardiac life that the mental body does not always comprehend and yet that palpitates in correspondence with the heart of the world, with the very life of the Word. It is through these channels that the heavens are revealed to us, that we are able to perceive indescribable beauties, and to believe unknowable truths.

While being a separate space, the kingdom of God, which is the house of the Father, is to be found everywhere. This antimony is one of the rapports that the absolute maintains with the relative realm. This mansion in fact contains many rooms, so that each kingdom of the relative world harbors within its core a premise wherein heaven is really and totally to be found, and wherein the Word dwells and works.

Jesus says "I am the way, the truth and the life" because he is the act, the goal, and the means; the law, knowledge, and the work; the path that leads to God, the vision of God, and the effort towards God. Those among you who appreciate lofty philosophy will be able to collate this text to the one where the shepherd Krishna speaks of himself in the *Bhagavad Gita*. Beneath outward similarities, they will discover, I hope, how the union described in the gospel (where the individuality remains intact) differs from Raja Yoga, where the individual immerses himself and is engulfed into the Universal Whole.

Between the Father and the Son there is neither fusion nor identity: there is communion. They are, together, such as noumenon and phenomenon, such as cause and effect, such as will and act. Christ is the organ, the voice, the hand of the Father. His works are the exact and perfect expression of the designs of God. Hence, if due to spiritual slackness, intellectual obscuration, or adverse education man does not adhere to the person of the Savior, it is sufficient for him to believe in the Savior's acts to recognize in them the seal, the stamp of the divine, of goodness, of verity, and of loftiness.

These acts are good, one might say, because they respond perfectly to the solicitation of circumstances and of witnesses. In fact, in proportion as creation unfolds, the horizons of intelligence and of the heart expand and their needs increase. Hence the disciple asks for more and more and for bigger and greater things. And he receives them, because he requests them in the name of our Lord Jesus Christ, of his merits, of his works and of his sufferings.

The Faithful Friend

It would not be honest to avail oneself of a protector to whom one does not feel bound; hence, obedience is the measure of love, and love without acts is but a fleeting fragrance.

The disciple strives to do his best; in return, the Master smiles at him. His smile is the Consoler. This is a strange being: the most mysterious, incomprehensible, subtle being. More accurately, it is we who remain extraneous to the Consoler because almost everything within us is but fallacy. Let us try to grasp this elusive ungraspable entity.

Truth, or Verity, exists as a supernatural and permanent individual. It is the intellectual form of the Word. The Word (if we dare express it so) possesses: a body, the kernel of which is the mystery of the human nature of our Lord Jesus Christ; a soul, which is his divine nature; a spirit, which is the Holy Spirit—the breath or wind, the exhalation, the aura, the halo, and the wake of divinity crossing the infinite abysses of all depths and heights.

Let us go further: "The Consoler instructs and recalls everything to your mind," says John 14:26.

Knowledge is a perfect perception disencumbered from any personal distortion resulting from our mental impurities, freed from any distortion of the milieu caused by the object to be studied, from any deformation of the object stemming from its actual appearance, which at the present time is relative.

Memory is the faculty of reviving an image of the past in spite of the disappearance of the cells that took it in. Grief arises from ignorance of life, from its secret resiliency, from its true causes, and from our obliviousness to the lights.

Therefore, a force that would give us continuously the exact notion of the mysterious connections between beings, of the true causation of events, that would maintain within us, to the quick, the remembrance of the blessed moment when heaven spoke to us—such a force would banish all fears from our path, would cleanse our atmosphere from all morbid ferments, would take us out of the limits of time, since the eternal splendor that appeared to us once upon a time would remain ever-present. Such a force would definitely be the Consoler.

Just as when a man speaks, the timbre of his voice is imbued with the spirit, the essence, of the ideas he expresses, so when he works the electrical aura of his muscles is colored similarly to the spirit of his act. When he walks the atmosphere behind him carries the odic traces of his movements. Hence each word, each thought, each action of Jesus determinates vibrations, breaths, radiations, that are the Spirit, the splendor of Verity, and the immutable witnesses of his vanished Presence in the future.

But only those who love him can, by means of his halo, find the vanished Master again. Temporal men have not yet developed within themselves the organ indispensable to this pursuit, nor to this vision.

The descent of the Spirit is similar to a second coming of the Word. Jesus placed a light in the physical world. Because it is alive, it spreads little by little into the very substance of beings. It opens the inner eye. It throws a light upon our intimate relationships with the Son, and upon those of the Son with the Father. This is the way the unification of man with God is effected. Thus do we obtain the freedom of the city within the celestial realm. Thus does Truth increase within us and develop as it sojourns in our personality. Thus do these mysterious faculties that the Church calls the gifts of the Holy Spirit (those we referred to when we spoke of

The Faithful Friend

the Trinity) get organized, those gifts which are as far above the transcendental faculties of the adepts of esoteric sciences as these latter surpass the ordinary faculties of man.

If the Father gives us *faith* by means of the regeneration of the will, if the Son gives us *charity* through the purification of the heart, and the Holy Spirit procures us *hope* by sublimating our mental state.

This is how Jesus Christ brings a light to the witnesses of his acts. Those witnesses assimilate it more or less according to the degree that their organs are qualified to receive it. The most important part of this process unfolds when the initiatory act has been accomplished within the unconscious regions of the man, because it is there that the Spirit operates. Until such time as the Holy Spirit intervenes, the disciples are able to understand only the outer significance of the words of the Master; only then do they discover their living and fecund depth, their useful applications, their live connections with the tangible world.

This is where one finds the veritable consolation, the true peace, that our Lord alone can give. What he offers his friends is one of the virtues he possesses, just as a *pater familias* entrusts his offspring to his most worthy servant, though he reserves for himself the worry, the anguish, and ruse. This is when the prince of this world, the Adversary of old, approaches: the Passion is now beginning.

This is where tears intermingle with joy in order to quicken one another reciprocally. The crushing and the death of the Innocent One means the triumph of heaven; the victor of this world has nothing more to expect. But he whom hell and the malice of men torments and tortures can rejoice because his agony marks the hour of a supernatural and definitive victory.

THE CROWNING OF HIS WORK

The Friends

JESUS DECLARED TO THOSE WHO FOLLOWED HIM: "I do not call you servants, but friends, because I have made known to you all that I learned from my Father." (John 15:15)

Now, a servant lives apart; he receives wages; he can change masters. A friend, on the other hand, does not expect a salary; his very wealthy Friend offers him presents as tokens of his affection, but not as compensation for his troubles; they live in close intimacy and are loyal to each other forever.

The servant has zeal, no doubt, to a certain extent; but it either warms up or weakens depending on his master's mood. The friend's zeal keeps on growing measurelessly; he does not obey the orders of a master; he loves his Friend ingenuously. For him, the word "duty" does not exist anymore since it is for love that he willingly labors gratuitously. To him all fatigues are bliss; he lives in a state of gladness without outer demonstrations, with profound and calm joy that radiates with power, but that alleviates all of the sorrows and sufferings around him.

These are the sentiments I wish you to hold on to. A great many among you fear God instead of loving him. You dread his ineffable conversation. You fear having to suffer more than your share because of your status as disciples. First of all, nothing is less certain, and secondly, you know that sufferings are always commensurate with our means of bearing them: the same painful ordeal might be insignificant to a man of strong character yet unbearable to a mollycoddle. Be more open with God; do not believe him to be mean or a haggler. If you feel restrained, constrained by his

The Faithful Friend

presence, it means that you are not sufficiently humble; that you are not true believers, nor sufficiently good. Keep reminding yourselves that there are no walls around your cloister, that no monastic rule guides you step by step. You have elected to be scouts, freelance disciples. In the person of Christ what struck you most was his loneliness, his isolation, his solitude. The salient nature of his being is unique. So keep the same courage in carrying out your vow as you did in pronouncing it.

Tell yourselves that you have to manage alone. The army of light includes both troops of occupation and troops of consolidation. You wanted to start on a voyage of discovery. Do not retrace your steps. Accost life calmly, with circumspection, especially with silent conciliation.

A frowning brow denotes one's fear of defeat; an impassive expression betrays the force of a demigod jaded with success; a smiling countenance portrays the irresistible innocent power of the mystical child whose spirit saturates powerlessness. Therefore, when you address people and things, do so good-naturedly, smilingly. Do not be surprised at anything. Let nothing startle you. Let no aspect of evil confound you. Try to understand everything, even the pettiness of people. It is essential that those who come to you be made to feel that regardless of their worries or their pain, you "have already been there and done that."

When a great test comes along, do not wallow in unhappiness or self-pity. That test, that ordeal, is the sole divine process for spiritual growth. An ordeal is the only real work testing our moral personality. Moreover, a test is the sole means to purify nature. Hence, experiencing the joy of being good laborers must be for us a time of rejoicing—it is a good training-ground for brave soldiers. We do not comprehend our happiness. Look around you; look at the hedonists settled in their sumptuous abodes, see the carnality of the pub-crawlers. Do you see any happy faces among them? Of course not. All the while these poor restless souls are saying they are happy, their facial expressions invalidate their words; while you, to the contrary, hold essential bliss in your hands—yet think yourself unhappy?

Focus your contemplations, rather, upon the splendor of the heavens on high. Jesus often speaks to you, but your moroseness prevents you from hearing him. Open the apertures of your being; cleanse yourselves; ask for the bliss of angels so as to share and spread it all about you without measure. You will soon notice how your radiation increases!

⊕

Christ exhorted his friends: "You shall have tribulations in the world, but take heart: I conquered the world."

But what is courage?

True courage is not about ignoring fear, but dominating it. Courage is not sudden bravado that takes away self-control; it is to retain our lucidity at the moment we are being precipitated towards death. Courage does not mean to experience collective inebriation; it means being heroic when no one is watching, when one is all alone in the night. True courage means to be on the ready at all times, by deploying moral bravery before moral danger, by deploying physical courage before physical danger, even when one is ill or feeble. In short, to face all circumstances squarely.

In order to face these spiritual obligations, we owe it to our ideal to employ but one single force: faith.

The Faithful Friend

Peace

AT A GIVEN TIME, EACH KINGDOM AMONG CREATURES may enjoy the peace that it has by right. It is a relative, external calm, a short slumber. Each one of our principles also takes a rest at intervals. But the peace Christ leaves us and gives his friends is a central, profound, immutable, and superhuman peace. It rules over humble hearts. It is wholly life, harmony, activity, certitude, and serenity. It is a diamond rock. The waves breaking against it do not abrade it, and the most raging tempest only serves to accentuate its pure, inalterable refulgence.

Inertia, apathy, indifference—and by contrast, vanity, self-sufficiency, and pride—bear no resemblance whatever to the peace of Christ. This peace is no more a passive feeling than is Christian resignation. On the contrary, it is positive, active, radiating. It is a virtue, which means a force.

Heaven means light, expansion, soaring. Its inhabitants always say "yes" to one another. Hell is obscurity, constriction, anguish, refusal. Rather than lament our errors and shortcomings, as soon as we have acknowledged them let us stride towards verity, which is Christ. Let us unite with him through thought, through love, and by acts.

Christ—the splendor of the Father who cherishes us with an inconceivable love, who desires nothing else but to be made welcome by us—we cannot receive with fear or sadness. Rather, we must lay ourselves open to his force and to his consolation. Let us cut anguish adrift, no matter how grave the causes may be. If our Master judges it right for us to enjoy human happiness and felicity, nothing is easier for him to do. If he judges it right for us to endure ordeals, what good is it to revolt? Why should we fear? Let us force ourselves to be confident, calm, and willing.

THE CROWNING OF HIS WORK

First of all, no fevered haste. The work we are performing at this moment according to the will of God is the one we have to finish first. Another occupation will come later. There must not be any impatience, not even against ourself. We must nurse neither scruples nor apprehensions. We must shed cupidity in the fields of money, of honors, books, sciences, and everything else. We must not live constrained, feel anxious, pessimistic, mistrustful, prying, or jealous. We must not veer towards boredom.

The great secret is to live totally in the will of God. We will discover his will in the thousand tasks our duties daily require; with it come the force and the light necessary to fulfill that will. All one needs is to accept, to love everything that presents itself, and to drop any extraneous desire that arises within us. Thus the will of God becomes our sole goal. Thereby we will perform each task carefully, patiently, with love and joy. We will not feel the need to hasten, or to be done, with any unpleasant job. Consequently, everything will become as easy for us as the frolic of a child at sunrise.

By offering heaven the means of installing itself in the hidden corners of our being, difficult chores will seem easy, since the difficulty springs from our powerlessness and pride. As the self diminishes, so heaven grows within us at the same time as security, optimism, and contentment increase. Just as the athlete judges the progress of his gymnastic exercises by the sensation of superabundant vigor that palpitates throughout his harmonious muscles, so the disciple will measure his mystical health by the permeating feelings of kindness and of strength that transport him beyond the lustreless horizons of the people on the outside.

Let us become accustomed to take into account our good

The Faithful Friend

fortunes rather than focus upon our bad luck; our minor elations, rather than our disappointments. Our nature induces us to see life with its problems and difficulties; instead, we should look for its facilities and enchantments. This way, we will reach the harbor that religious writers call the state of indifference. But in our contemporary language this signifies something dry, frozen—which does not correspond at all to the disciple's state of soul.

To me it seems preferable to describe this psychological disposition as "inner peace" that enables us to be acutely interested in everything without being bound to anything; that prevents us from ever feeling anything to be thwarting; that, finally, is the sign of the greatest flexibility of character, energy, intelligence, or sensibility in the human being, and that at the same time is the sign of the greatest stability in the center of our heart, flawlessly bound to Christ.

That inner peace must radiate without.

Whoever, whatever, comes our way, let us welcome it with an open heart and with benevolence. Whether derelicts, vagrants, or millionaires, whether hovels or palaces, pleasant landscapes or desert sands, sun or tempest—nothing is totally ugly, nothing is totally beautiful. Each thing, each creature, is a more or less distorted reflection of an eternal splendor. We may not perceive this beam of light, but let us realize that it exists. Let us be blind to impoliteness, deaf to malicious gossip, insensible to rudeness. Let us give to each creature whatever we are able to offer, such as: our time, taste, money, affability, knowledge, experience. Let us love all beings as Jesus loved them.

Thus will we live at peace with the world.

Everything is a bounty from God; hence, to the disciple, everything becomes a motive for rejoicing. From the very inception of the world up to its very end, God singles us out, identifies us, watches over us, loves us immeasurably. Why should we not be blissful and feel blessed?

So we must react against the ingrained habits of discontent, complaints, strategic laziness, by forcing ourselves to welcome everything with an open, smiling countenance. In fact, everything is a blessing from the Father; everything is an occasion for showing our confidence; everything is a motive to love him, to serve him better; everything may be of use and serve our fellowmen—and if we want it so, everything becomes an additional step closer to heaven.

The Testament of the Friend

WE ARE UNAWARE OF THE MYSTERY THAT THE VEGEtable kingdom hides, and of how closely woven is its life to that of the Spirit. The plant is the creature that realizes best the law of love. Observe how its roots, vessels, ducts, and cells develop, how it produces its flowers, fruits, and seeds. In the world of spirits (as closely as words can approximate or correspond to a precise meaning within us), the Father is the wine-grower, the Son is the vine-stock, and we men are the vine-shoots. We can live only by adhering to the vine-stock; when separated from it, our life is but a death.

Unless we work, we die, since we are not of any further use to the vine-stock, to the sapling to which we belong; so we pass into winter through the fire of proving; and the ashes we leave behind in its crucible, mixed with the soil again, have another long course to pursue before becoming a part of a vine-stock anew.

When we work, other tests arise to sublimate us; and so we reach a higher sphere of life, just as the substance of the

The Faithful Friend

vine incorporates itself within man under the form of wine. But for this to happen the vine-shoots must live from the life of the vine-stock. That is what Christ recommends when he says: "Abide in me." (John 15:4–10)

Then life abounds, our demands are granted, our works are blessed, and from perfect obedience to the organic law of our spiritual being is born that particular perfect joy that resplendently radiates from all those who have received the peace of Christ. We have then become faithful servants, conscious collaborators, friends of God.

What is the purpose of the life of the Word? It is to give himself to the world. To partake of his life, let us give ourselves to the small fraction of the world with which we are in contact. Logically, it follows that those who are attached to the principle of selfishness will attack and persecute us.

Let us bless these adversaries. Are they not the best pedagogues one can find to learn how to love? What is simpler than to give to people we like? To consecrate our time and care for antipathetic people is heroism in the bud; to sacrifice ourselves for those who hate us, is divine. First, never hate those who love us, but love them; neither be hostile or indifferent towards those whom we feel to be indifferent; we must neither hate, nor remain indifferent, but love our enemies—these are the seven stages of charity.

Charity is the universal school. Nowhere does Christ recommend study. After all, why are we ignorant? Because our mind does not open, our memory fails, our attention vacillates, our reasoning deviates, our judgment grows warped, our conceptions shrink, our intuition clouds over. All these infirmities come from the self. It is the self that restricts our inner horizons, that withers our forces, that renders us obtuse, obstinate, biased, worrisome, and sick.

THE CROWNING OF HIS WORK

Whoever has transmuted his inner selfishness ceases to be an enemy to any being. Not being feared anymore, other beings come to him. All he has to do is ask a question for the spirits of creatures to reveal their secrets to him. And the truth hidden within the center of any being, whether it be in a stone, a elemental spirit, a concept, an abstraction, or an event, will reveal itself to him. This is the way the Spirit of Truth functions. To such a man, books as well as intellect become useless. Being one in Christ in his heart and in his whole personality, it is not he who works or asks anymore, it is the Word. From then on he knows everything and can do anything.

As for us, only from time to time does a thousandth part of our individuality perform some good; remember: selfishness is at the origin of our powerlessness and of our ignorance.

The man having attained such a stable state of abnegation lives from eternal life wherever he is, were it even in the depths of hell. Yet he has done nothing but obey progressively according to the knowledge of the law that was being revealed to him. That is how he came to recognize what comes from God, from the devil, or from nature. He augments the glory of the Word, and in return the Word looks after him, for the Father helps him to resist until the end, suffering gladly, yet preserved from internal evil.

Truth sanctifies this man. He becomes one of its sparks, because Truth is life, and it is with the perspective of this transmutation that the Word came on earth. This faithful servant transmits the words of the law to others; but all of them, from the first to the last, may become, if they want to, one sole being: by uniting in obedience to their common Master.

The Faithful Friend

This is what the Word came to accomplish—to launch into the world the seed of such a union, of a harmony similar to the one that reigns in heaven. His disciples draw their very existence, their life from him; living off his force, they are wherever he is; and he is everywhere they are. Ineffable deliverance that neither the will nor science can produce, but that Love alone operates.

PART IV

The Crowning of His Work

FTER SINGING the Psalms, they set out to the Mount of Olives. Jesus then said to his disciples: "Tonight, you will all lose courage because of me. For it is written: I will smite the shepherd, and the sheep of the flock will be scattered. But after my resurrection, I will precede you to Galilee." Peter answered: "Though all men would lose courage because of you, I shall never fail you!" Jesus continued: "Simon, Simon! See how satan has claimed all of you to sift you like wheat; but I have prayed for you Peter, so that your faith does not fail. And you, once you shall have been converted, strengthen your brothers!" Peter retorted: "Lord, I am prepared to go to prison and to die with you." Jesus replied: "Peter, I am telling you that today, this very night, before the cock crows, you will have denied me three times!" But Peter vehemently insisted: "No, even though I should have to die with you, I shall not deny you!" And everyone said the same.

After that, Jesus asked them: "When I sent you without purse, bag, or sandals, did you want for anything?" "Nothing!" they answered. "But now," said Jesus, "if you have a purse, take it, and also a bag; and if you don't have a sword, sell your cloak to buy one. For it is written: And he was numbered with the transgressors. And I tell you that this must be fulfilled in me. Yes, what is written about me is reaching its fulfillment."

The disciples said, "See Lord, there are two swords." He answered: "That is enough."

THE CROWNING OF HIS WORK

After having spoken thus, Jesus went with his disciples beyond the stream of Cedron to the Mount of Olives. There was the garden Gethsemane, which he entered with them. Judas, who betrayed him, knew this place well, for Jesus and his disciples used to go there regularly. Then Jesus told his disciples: "Sit down here while I go over there to pray."

So he took with him Peter, James, and John. As he fell into a state of prostration, agony overcame him. He told his companions: "My soul is saddened even unto death! Stay here, watch with me! Pray not to succumb to the ordeal."

He walked about a stone's throw away from them; there, having knelt down, he prostrated himself, his face to the ground, and prayed that, were it possible, this hour might pass from him: "My Father! everything is possible for you! If you would only take away this cup from me! Nevertheless, not what I will but what you will."

He returned to his disciples, and found them asleep. "What!" said he to Peter, "are you asleep? Were you not able to watch a single hour with me? Get up! Watch and pray so that you do not succumb to the ordeal; for the spirit is full of eagerness, but the flesh is weak."

He left them for the second time and prayed saying: "My Father, if it is not possible for this cup to pass without my drinking of it, may your will be done!"

He came back to them and found them asleep, weary with sorrow; their eyes were heavy with sleep and they did not know what to reply.

He left them again and prayed for the third time:

The Crowning of His Work

"Father, if only you wanted to take this cup from me! Nevertheless, not my will, but your will."

Then an angel having come from heaven appeared to strengthen him.

In agony, he kept on praying more earnestly, and his sweat, like drops of blood, fell to the ground.

After having prayed, he got up, went back to his disciples and told them: "Sleep now and rest! It is enough! The hour has come! See, the Son of Man is delivered into the hands of sinners. Wake up! Let us go! The one who betrays me is already approaching."

⊕

While he was still speaking, Judas, one of the Twelve, appeared, and with him a multitude armed with swords and staves. Judas had led the cohort and agents provided by the chiefs of the priests, the Pharisees, the scribes, and the elders of the people. Thus he came to this place with lanterns, torches, and weapons.

Jesus, knowing all that was to happen to him, moved forward and said to them: "Who are you looking for?" "Jesus of Nazareth." "It is I!" In the midst of them stood Judas, the one who was delivering him.

Hardly had Jesus said to them: "It is I!" than they fell backwards to the ground.

He asked them a second time: "Who are you looking for?"

They said: "Jesus of Nazareth." Jesus reiterated: "I have told you it is I; if you are really looking for me, let these people go." This was in order that the word he had spoken would be fulfilled: "I have lost none of those whom you have given me."

THE CROWNING OF HIS WORK

However the traitor had agreed to give them a signal: the one whom I shall kiss, it is he; seize him and take him away. So he went up to Jesus and said "Hail, Master!" And kissed him.

But Jesus said: "Judas, what brings you here? Is it with a kiss that you betray the Son of Man?"

They laid hands on Jesus.

Those who surrounded him, seeing what was going to happen, asked him: "Lord, shall we strike with the sword?" And one of them, Simon Peter, stretched out his hand, drew his sword, struck the servant of the high-priest and took off his right ear. This servant's name was Malchus.

Jesus said: "Stop! wait!" Then he touched the ear of the servant and healed it. And addressing Peter: "Put your sword back into the sheath, for those who take the sword shall perish by the sword. Shall I not drink the cup which the Father has given me to drink? Do you not think that I could invoke my Father, who would send more than twelve legions of angels to my aid at this very moment? But then, how would the Scriptures be fulfilled wherein it is foretold that it must be so?"

Then he said to the multitude, the chief priests, the officers of the temple, and the elders who had risen against him: "You have come out with swords and staves to take me as if I were a thief. Yet I was with you every day teaching in the temple and you did not lay hands on me! But this is your hour and the power of darkness. All of this has happened so that the writings of the prophets may be fulfilled!"

The disciples left him and fled. Alone, a certain

The Crowning of His Work

young man was following him, having but a light cloth on his body. He was seized; so, leaving the cloth in the hands of the guards, he ran away naked.

⊕

The cohort, the tribune, and the agents of the Jews took Jesus and pinioned him. First they began by leading him to Annas, father-in-law to Caiaphas, who was the high-priest that year. This was the Caiaphas who had given this counsel to the Jews: It is better that one man should die for the people.

Simon Peter and another disciple were following Jesus from afar; this disciple, who was known to the high-priest, entered the courtyard at the same time as Jesus. As for Peter, he remained outside by the door. The other disciple, who was known to the high-priest, then left; he spoke to the doorkeeper and brought Peter in. Peter came in and sat down to see how it would end.

It was cold. The slaves and the servants stood around a brazier that they had lit in the middle of the courtyard in order to warm themselves. Peter was with them, warming himself, too.

The maidservant, who was the doorkeeper, seeing Peter seated in the firelight, looked closely at him and said: "Are you not also one of the disciples of this man?" "No, not I," he replied.

As he was going out towards the door, another servant saw him and said to those who were there: "This man was with Jesus the Nazarene." Peter denied it again with an oath: "I do not know this man at all!"

THE CROWNING OF HIS WORK

After an interval of about an hour, another asserted the fact saying: "It is true! This man was also with him, for he is a Galilean!"

Some bystanders approached and said to Peter: "Of course you too are one of them, for your manner of speaking betrays you!" One of the servants of the chief priest, a relative of the one whose ear Peter had cut off, added: "Did I not see you in the garden with him? You too are one of them!" So he began to curse and swore: "I do not know this man, and I do not know what you mean!"

At that very moment, while he was still speaking, a cock crowed. The Lord turned around and looked at Peter. Then Peter remembered the word of the Lord and how he had told him: Before the cock crows today, you will deny me three times!

He went outside and wept bitterly.

⊕

However the high-priest questioned Jesus about his disciples and his teachings.

Jesus answered: "I have spoken openly to the world; I have always taught in the synagogue and within the walls of the temple where all the Jews usually assemble, and I have said nothing in secret. Why are you questioning me? Ask those who have heard me how I spoke; they know well what I have said."

At these words, one of the bailiffs next to him struck him on the face saying: "Is this how you answer the high-priest?"

Jesus addressed this man: "If I have spoken badly,

show me what I have said wrong; if I have spoken well, why do you strike me?"

But the men who held Jesus mocked him, struck him, and spat upon him. After having put a veil on his head, they struck his face saying: "Guess, Christ! Who has struck you?"

The men-servants greeted him by cudgelling him and heaping abuse upon him.

Then Annas sent him bound to Caiaphas the high-priest.

⊕

At daybreak, the chief priests, the elders of the people, the scribes, the whole Sanhedrin gathered. They brought Jesus before the court and spoke to him thus: "If you are the Christ, tell us!"

He answered "Even were I to tell you, you would not believe me; and if I questioned you, you would not answer me!"

The whole Sanhedrin sought evidence against Jesus that would condemn him to death; but they found none. For many bore false witness against him and their depositions were contradictory. Finally there appeared some who brought against him this false testimony: "We have heard him say: I shall destroy this sanctuary made by the hands of men and in three days I will build another one which will not be made by the hands of men."

But even on this point their depositions did not agree. So the high-priest rose up in the middle of the council and questioned Jesus: "Are you not answering

THE CROWNING OF HIS WORK

to the testimonies these people are making against you?" But Jesus remained silent; he answered not a word.

A second time, the high-priest questioned him: "In the name of the living God, I beseech you: Tell us if you are Christ, the Son of the blessed God!" "You have spoken!" replied Jesus. "And furthermore I declare unto you, from now on you shall see the Son of Man seated on the right of the almightiness of God and coming on the clouds of the heavens!"

They all said with one voice: "Then you are the Son of God? He replied: "I am he!"

Then the high-priest tore his garments and said: "He has blasphemed! We need no further witness! You have heard this blasphemy yourselves! What do you make of it?"

The whole crowd arose: "We have heard it from his own lips!"

Consequently, everyone condemned him as deserving death.

After having bound him, they led Jesus away and delivered him to Pilate, the governor.

⊕

However, Judas who had betrayed him, seeing that Jesus was condemned, felt remorse for what he had done and took the thirty pieces of silver to the chiefs of the priests and the elders, saying: "I was wrong to deliver an innocent man"! They replied: "What is that to us! It is your affair!" But, after having thrown the pieces of silver into the temple, he went away and hanged himself.

The Crowning of His Work

As for the chiefs of the priests, they took the silver and said: "It is not permitted to put this money into the sacred treasury, for it is the price of blood."

Having held counsel, they bought with it the Potter's Field for the burial of strangers. Hence the name of Field-of-Blood, as it is still called today.

Thus it is that the words of the prophet were fulfilled: "They received the thirty pieces of silver, the price of the one who had been valued at this price by the sons of Israel; and they gave it for the Potter's Field according to the order that I had received from the Lord."

⊕

The members of the Sanhedrin then took Jesus from Caiaphas' home to the Praetorium.

Day was dawning.

The Jews themselves did not go into the Praetorium so as not to be sullied and defiled and to be able to eat the Passover. Pilate came to them, outside. "What accusation do you bring against this man?" said he. They answered: "Were he not a wrongdoer, we would not have delivered him to you!"

Pilate replied: "Take him yourselves and judge him according to your law!" "We do not have the right to sentence to death," retorted the Jews.

Thus were fulfilled the words which Jesus had spoken to indicate the kind of death he was to undergo.

So they began accusing him: "We have found this man inciting our people to revolt and deterring them from paying tribute to Caesar, calling himself Christ-the-king!"

Hence, Pilate went back into the Praetorium, had Jesus brought before the court, and said to him: "You are the king of the Jews?"

Jesus answered: "Are you saying this on your own or have others told you this about me?" "Am I a Jew? Me!" retorted Pilate.

"Your nation and the chief priests have handed you over to me; what have you done?"

"My kingdom is not of this world," replied Jesus. "If my kingdom were of this world, my subjects would have fought so that I would not be given over to the Jews; but my kingship is not of this world."

Pilate asked him: "So you are a king?"

Jesus replied: "So you say, I am a king. I was born for that, and for that I have come into the world so as to bear witness to the truth. Whoever is in the truth listens to my voice."

Pilate asked him: "What is truth?"

As soon as he had uttered these words he again went out to the Jews and said to them: "I can find no crime in this man, no reason for condemnation."

As the chief priests were formulating all kinds of accusations against Jesus, who made no reply, Pilate questioned him again: "Why do you not answer? Do you not hear what you are accused of?"

But Jesus gave no more reply; at which Pilate was very surprised.

However, the Jews persisted more and more and said: "He was provoking the people by teaching throughout Judea, and it is after having begun in Galilee that he has reached as far as here!"

At the word of Galilee, Pilate asked if the man were

The Crowning of His Work

Galilean. Informed that he was a subject of Herod, he sent him back to Herod, who happened to be in Jerusalem at that time.

⊕

Seeing Jesus was a great satisfaction to Herod. He had wished to know him for some time because he had heard of him and hoped to see him perform some miracle. Therefore he questioned him at length. But Jesus made no reply to him.

As for the chief priests and the scribes, they were there, standing up, plaguing him with their accusations. But Herod, with his guards, paid no more attention to Jesus; out of derision, he arrayed him in a white robe and sent him back to Pilate.

Pilate and Herod, who were enemies until then, became friends from that time on.

Later, Pilate, having gathered together the chief priests, the magistrates, and the people, made this speech to them: "You have presented this man to me as an agitator; but, having examined him myself before you, I have not found this man guilty of any of the crimes of which you are accusing him. Neither does Herod, for he has sent him back to us. Therefore, he has done nothing which deserves death. After having chastised him, I shall then set him free."

⊕

At the time of each feast of the Passover, the governor had the custom of granting the Jews the release of a prisoner, the one they asked for. At this time there was a well-known prisoner named Bar-Abbas, who was

THE CROWNING OF HIS WORK

held with his accomplices for a murder and for an insurrection that had taken place in the town.

The crowd went up to the tribunal and began asking Pilate for the usual grace. When they had assembled, Pilate said to them: "Which one would you like me to release: Bar-Abbas, or Jesus, who is called Christ? Would you like me to release the king of the Jews?"

For he knew that it was out of envy that the chief priests had surrendered Jesus to him.

At that moment, as he was sitting on the tribunal, his wife sent him a message: "Do not intervene in the case of this just man, for today I have been greatly tormented in a dream because of him."

For their part, the chief priests and the elders incited the crowd and persuaded it to ask for Bar-Abbas and to have Jesus put to death. The governor repeated his question: "Which of the two would you like me to release?" And they all shouted with one voice: "Bar-Abbas! Not this man, but Bar-Abbas! Take away this man! Release Bar-Abbas to us!"

And yet Bar-Abbas was a thief.

Pilate, wishing to free Jesus, addressed them again: "What would you like me to do with the one whom you call the king of the Jews, Jesus, known as the Christ?" Everyone cried out: "Crucify, crucify him!"

For the third time he said to them: "But what wrong has he done? I have found nothing in him deserving death. Therefore, after having chastised him, I will release him."

But they insisted with loud cries, demanding that he be crucified; and the clamor rose, intensified...

Upon seeing that he was achieving nothing, but that

The Crowning of His Work

the tumult was increasing, Pilate, wishing to satisfy the crowd, pronounced a judgment in accordance with their demand. At their request, he released Bar-Abbas, who had been put into prison for insurrection and for murder, and he ordered Jesus to be seized and to be scourged.

The soldiers of the governor took him inside the court, which is the Praetorium, and assembled the entire cohort. After having undressed him, they decked out Jesus in a military cloak red in color; then they wove a crown of thorns and put it on his head, as well as a reed in his right hand; and, bowing their knees before him, they said to him out of derision: "Hail, king of the Jews!" Then they slapped his face, spat upon him, and, taking the reed, they beat him on the head.

"See, I am bringing him outside for you, so that you will know that I find no reason to condemn him."

Jesus indeed appeared, wearing the crown of thorns and the crimson cloak. And Pilate said to them: "Here is the man."

When the chief priests and their people caught sight of him, they began to shout: "Crucify, crucify him!"

Pilate told them: "Take him yourselves then, and crucify him; I find in him no reason to condemn him." The Jews replied: "And we have a law, and according to our law, he must die, because he has declared himself to be the Son of God!"

So when Pilate heard these words, he became more and more afraid. He went back into the Praetorium and asked Jesus this question: "Where do you come from?"

THE CROWNING OF HIS WORK

But Jesus gave no reply.

Pilate continued: "Will you not speak to me? Do you not know that I have the power to crucify you, and that I have the power to release you?"

Jesus answered him: "You would have no power over me had it not been given to you from above. That is why the one who hands me over to you is guilty of a greater sin." Whereupon Pilate made an effort to release him. But the Jews kept shouting to him: "If you release this man, you are not a friend of Caesar; for whoever makes himself a king declares himself against Caesar!"

Upon hearing this harangue, Pilate had Jesus brought outside, and sat down at the tribunal, at the place called the Mosaic Pavement, in Hebrew: Gabbatha. It was the day before the Passover, at about the sixth hour (midday).

Pilate told the Jews: "Here is your king!" But they clamored: "Take him away! Take him away! Crucify him!" "Would I crucify your king?" The chief priests replied: "We have no other king than Caesar!"

Then Pilate asked for some water and washed his hands before the people, saying: "I am innocent of the blood of this man. It is up to you to answer for it!" "May his blood be upon us and upon our children!" replied the people.

Upon which, Pilate handed Jesus over to them to be crucified.

The soldiers took off the crimson cloak and put his own robes back on. Then they took Jesus and led him away...

The Crowning of His Work

⊕

He was taken outside to be crucified. Carrying his cross himself, Jesus was led to the place called Calvary, in Hebrew: Golgotha.

As they led him away, they requisitioned a passer-by who was returning from the fields, a man from Cyrene named Simon, the father of Alexander and of Rufus. They made him shoulder the cross to carry it behind Jesus. A large crowd of people was following him, and women who were lamenting and weeping over him.

"Daughters of Jerusalem," Jesus, facing them, said, "Do not weep for me, but weep for yourselves and for your children! For days are coming when it will be said: Blessed are the sterile, blessed are the wombs that have not given birth and the breasts that have not given milk! Then people will begin to say to the mountains: Fall upon us! And to the hills: Conceal us! For if green wood is dealt with in this way, what will happen to the dry wood?"

They were taking along two other men, robbers, to put them to death with him.

They arrived at the place called Golgotha, which means: the place of the skull. They gave him some wine mixed with myrrh to drink; after having tasted it, he refused to drink any more.

Then they crucified him along with the wrongdoers; one to the right, the other to the left, and Jesus in the middle.

"Father," said he, "forgive them, for they know not what they do!"

In order to indicate the reason for his condemna-

THE CROWNING OF HIS WORK

tion, Pilate also drafted an inscription and had it placed on the cross above the head of Jesus. It read:

JESUS OF NAZARETH, KING OF THE JEWS

Many Jews read this inscription, because the place where Jesus was crucified was near the town and because it was written in Hebrew, Greek, and Latin.

The chief priests said to Pilate: "Do not put: king of the Jews, but: This man has said: I am the king of the Jews."

Pilate replied: "What I have written, I have written!"

However, after having crucified Jesus, the soldiers took his clothes and divided them into four shares, one share each. They also took the tunic, but this tunic was without seams, made of a single piece of cloth from top to bottom. "Let us not tear it, they said among themselves, but let us cast lots as to who shall have it!"

Thus were fulfilled the words of the Scriptures: "They divide my clothes among themselves, and for my clothing they cast lots" [Psalm 22:18]. That is what the soldiers did. Then, to guard him, they sat there. The people also stood around and looked.

The passers-by insulted him, nodding their heads: "Hail! you who destroys the temple and rebuilds it in three days, save yourself if you are the Son of God! Come down from the cross!" Similarly, the chief priests, the scribes, and the elders also made fun of him and said: "He has saved the others and he cannot save himself! Ah, Ah—Christ! God's chosen one! The king of Israel! Let him now come down from the cross and we will believe in him, for he has said: I am the Son of God!" And the soldiers also went up to make fun of

The Crowning of His Work

him; and they offered him vinegar, saying: "If you are the king of the Jews, save yourself!"

One of the crucified robbers kept insulting him: "Are you not the Christ? Save yourself and us, too!"

But the other one raised his voice to reprove him: "Do you not fear God, you who are undergoing the same condemnation? For us it is justice, for we are getting what our acts deserve, but this man has done no wrong." Then he said to Jesus: "Lord, remember me when you come into your kingdom."

Jesus replied: "Verily I say to you, today you shall be with me in paradise!"

Meanwhile, at the foot of the cross, were standing the mother of Jesus, his mother's sister, Mary, wife of Cleopas, and Mary Magdalene.

Jesus saw his mother; then, next to her, the disciple whom he loved: "Woman, this is your son." To the disciple, he then said: "This is your mother!" From that moment on, the disciple took her to his home.

The sun dimmed and darkness fell upon the whole country until the ninth hour (three o'clock).

At the ninth hour, Jesus gave a great cry and called "Eloi! Eloi! lamma sabachtani!" which means: My God! My God! why have you forsaken me?"

Some of those present having heard him, said: "Look at him calling Elijah! Wait, let us see if Elijah will come to deliver him!"

After that, knowing that everything was going to be consummated so that the Scriptures would be fulfilled, Jesus said: "I am thirsty!"

Close by was a jar full of vinegar. Immediately, someone ran to fetch a sponge, filled it with vinegar,

THE CROWNING OF HIS WORK

fixed it onto a branch of hyssop, and put it to his mouth.

When Jesus had taken the vinegar, he said: "Everything has been fulfilled."

Then he cried out in a loud voice: "Father, I commend to you my spirit!"

And, bowing his head, he died.

Immediately, the veil of the temple tore in two from top to bottom; the earth shook, rocks cracked, sepulchers opened up, several of the saints who were dead rose in their bodies and came out of their graves. After the resurrection of Jesus, they entered into the holy city and appeared to many people.

However, the centurion who was facing Jesus, seeing that he had died uttering such a cry, glorified God, saying: "Without a doubt, this man was innocent."

Those who were guarding Jesus with him, terrorized by the earthquake and by everything that was happening, cried out: "Assuredly, this man was the Son of God!"

And the mob that had rushed up en masse to this spectacle, being witness of what had taken place, turned back beating their breasts.

As for the people he had known, they were standing at a distance, watching; so did the women who had followed Jesus from Galilee and who served him: Mary Magdalene, Mary, mother of James the Lesser and of Joses, Salome, mother of the sons of Zebedee, and many others who had made the journey from Jerusalem with him. They watched from afar.

This day happened to be the eve of a particularly solemn sabbath. So that the bodies would not remain

The Crowning of His Work

on the cross during the sabbath, the Jews came to ask Pilate to have the legs of the executed men broken and to have them taken down.

So the soldiers came and broke the legs of the first, and then of the other one who was crucified with him. But when they came to Jesus they saw that he was dead, and did not break his legs; however, one of the soldiers pierced his side with a spear and immediately blood and water came out of it.

The person who saw this testified to it and his testimony is true. He knows that he is telling the truth, so that you, too, shall have faith.

These things did happen so that these words of the Scriptures might be fulfilled: "None of his bones shall be broken."

Elsewhere, the Scripture also says: "They shall look upon him whom they had pierced."

⊕

It was getting late. A rich man, named Joseph of Arimathea in Judea, was an esteemed member of the Council. Being a good and just man, he had not agreed with the decision or the action of his colleagues. He, too, was awaiting the Kingdom of God, and he was even a disciple of Jesus, but in secret, out of fear of the Jews.

He went boldly to present himself before Pilate and asked his permission to take the body of Jesus.

Pilate was surprised that he was already dead. He called for the centurion to find out from him how long Jesus had been dead.

Having heard the report of the commander of the

guards, he ordered that the body be handed over to Joseph.

Joseph bought a shroud and went to Calvary. With him went Nicodemus, the one who, earlier, had visited Jesus during the night. He also brought about a hundred pounds of myrrh and aloes.

So they took the body of Jesus down from the cross, wrapped it in the cloths with the spices, as it is the custom of the Jews for burial, and placed him in a clean shroud.

At the site where he had been crucified, there was a garden, and in this garden a new tomb, which Joseph had had hewn out of the rock for himself, where nobody had yet been put. As it was the day before the sabbath and the tomb was near, they put Jesus in it.

Joseph rolled a large stone across the entrance to the tomb and went away.

Mary Magdalene, Mary, mother of Joses, and the women who had come from Galilee with Jesus, had followed him. They were there, sitting facing the tomb, observing it to see how the body was put in it. Then they went back to prepare the spices and perfumes. The sabbath was about to begin.

⊕

The next day (which was the day after the Preparation) the chief priests and the Pharisees went together to Pilate and said to him: "Lord, we have remembered that, when he was alive, this imposter said: After three days, I will rise. Order, therefore, that the tomb be carefully watched until the third day, for fear that his disciples come and steal the body and then say to the

The Crowning of His Work

people: He has risen from the dead. A final deception which would be worse than the first." Pilate answered them: "You have guards; go, stand watch as you see fit." So they went and secured the tomb, sealing the stone in the presence of the guards.

⊕

When the sabbath had passed, suddenly a violent earthquake erupted; for an angel of the Lord, come from heaven, went to the stone, rolled it away, and sat on it. He looked like lightning and his garments were as white as snow. The guards, seized with fear, trembled and became as dead.

Some went back into the town and announced to the chief priests all that had happened. The latter, after having met with the elders and held counsel, gave the soldiers a large sum of money with this order: "Say: His disciples came to steal him during the night while we were asleep. If the governor hears of it, we shall appease him and shall save you from punishment."

The soldiers took the money and followed the instructions they had been given. Thus has this rumor spread amongst the Jews to this day.

⊕

However, on the first day of the week, Mary Magdalene went to the tomb early in the morning before dawn. She saw the stone removed from the entrance to the vault. She ran immediately to find Simon Peter and the other disciple whom Jesus loved, and she said to them: "They have taken the Lord from his tomb and we do not know where they have put him."

THE CROWNING OF HIS WORK

✥

At dawn, John, Mary, mother of James, Salome, and the others came to visit the tomb, carrying the spices they had prepared. They said among themselves: "Who will roll the stone away for us from in front of the entrance to the sepulcher?"

Raising their eyes, they saw that the stone, which was very large, had been rolled aside. They entered, but they did not find the body of the Lord. They were filled with consternation.

But then they caught sight of a young man; he was seated to the right and dressed in a white robe. They were filled with terror and lowered their eyes to the ground: "Do not be afraid!" said he, "You are looking for Jesus of Nazareth who was crucified; why are you looking for the living among the dead? Jesus is not here; he has risen as he had said. Look at the place where he was put, and remember what he told you when he was still in Galilee: The Son of Man must be delivered into the hands of sinners, he must be crucified, and he must rise again on the third day!"

Then they remembered the words of Jesus.

They went out, they fled from the tomb with great joy, mingled with fear, as they had been seized with trembling and fright. At first, they told no one; they were afraid. Then they ran to give the news to the disciples, who took these words for reveries and did not want to believe them.

✥

For their part, Peter and the other disciple had gone out straightaway to go to the sepulcher. Both began to

The Crowning of His Work

run. More agile than Peter, the other disciple took the lead. He reached the tomb first; he leaned over, saw the cloths on the ground; however, he did not enter.

Then Simon Peter, who was following him, arrived. He went inside the tomb. He looked at the cloths which were on the ground, and saw that the shroud which had been on his head was not mixed with the cloths, but folded up in a separate place.

Then the other disciple, the one who had reached the sepulcher first, also went in; he saw and he believed. Until then, indeed, they had not understood the Scripture where it is said: He must rise from among the dead.

So the disciples went back home, amazed at what had taken place.

⊕

Mary had remained at the entrance to the sepulcher and was crying. In tears, she bent over and looked inside the tomb. There she saw two angels clothed in white seated, one at the head and the other at the foot of the place where the body of Jesus had lain. They asked her: "Woman, why are you crying?" She answered: "Because they have taken away my Lord, and I do not know where they have put him."

As she spoke, she turned around and saw Jesus standing behind her; but she was not aware that it was Jesus. Jesus said to her: "Woman, why are you crying? Who are you looking for?" Thinking it was the gardener, she replied: "Sir, if it is you who have taken him away, tell me where you have put him and I will go and look for him!" Jesus spoke to her: "Mary!" Turning

THE CROWNING OF HIS WORK

around, she said to him in Hebrew: "Rabboni!" which means "Master!" Jesus added: "Do not touch me, for I have not yet risen to my Father; but go to my brothers, and tell them that I am going up to my Father and your Father, to my God and your God!"

Mary Magdalene went to impart the news to the disciples: "I have seen the Lord and this is what he told me!"

⊕

That same day, two of the disciples were going to a market town called Emmaus, situated sixty stages (about eleven kilometers) away from Jerusalem. They were talking about what had just happened. While they were conversing and discussing, Jesus himself approached them and began talking with them; but a sort of fascination prevented their eyes from recognizing him. "What are you discoursing about and exchanging with each other as you walk; why are you sad?" he asked them. One of them, named Cleopas, answered: "You are indeed the only stranger here in Jerusalem who does not know of the things that have been happening there these days!" "About what?" he asked. "About Jesus of Nazareth, a powerful prophet in deeds and words before God and before all the people; how the chief priests and our magistrates delivered him to be condemned to death and crucified him. As for us, we were hoping that it was he who was to liberate Israel; but besides that, these things happened three days ago. It is true that some women of our entourage have greatly surprised us; having been at the tomb early in the morning, they did not find his body and

The Crowning of His Work

came back saying that they had even seen an apparition of angels. These were supposed to have told them that he is alive! Some of us went to the tomb; they did indeed find things as the women had said, but they did not see him at all!" "Oh foolish ones," said Jesus to them. "Oh hearts slow to believe all that the prophets have said! Was it not necessary for Christ to suffer all these things to enter into his glory?" And, beginning with Moses and all the prophets, he explained to them what throughout the Scriptures concerned him.

As they approached the town they were going to, Jesus seemed to want to go further. But they stopped him. "Stay with us," they said, "evening is falling nigh, it is twilight already."

He went in to stay with them. As they were at table together, he took the bread, pronounced the blessing, broke it, and gave it to them. Suddenly their eyes were opened; they recognized him. But he had disappeared from in front of them. Then they said to one another: "Was not our heart burning within us as he was speaking to us on the way, when he was explaining the Scriptures?"

And, getting up, on the spot they returned to Jerusalem; they found the Eleven and their companions assembled, who were saying: "The Lord has truly risen! He appeared to Simon!" They then related what had happened to them on the way, and how they had recognized him when he had broken the bread.

⊕

They were speaking thus, and the doors of the place had been bolted for fear of the Jews, when Jesus stood in the midst of them and said to them: "Peace be with you!"

Struck with amazement and fear, they thought they were seeing a spirit.

"Why are you troubled?" he said to them, "and why this hesitation in your hearts? See my hands and my feet; it is indeed I! Touch me, look at me; a spirit has neither flesh nor bones as you see I have!"

While speaking, he showed them his hands and his side. And, as, in their joy, they were still hesitating, confused, and agitated by the surprise: "Have you something to eat?" Jesus said to them.

They offered him a piece of roast fish. He took it and ate it in front of them. Then he added: "These are the words I was saying to you when I was still with you, that everything that has been written about me in the law of Moses and in the prophets and in the psalms must be fulfilled."

Then he enlightened their minds to make them understand the Scriptures. "Thus it is written that Christ must suffer and rise from among the dead on the third day; and that repentance and the remission of sins must be preached in his name to all nations, beginning with Jerusalem. You are witnesses to these things. I shall send down upon you what my Father has promised. And you shall remain in the town until you have been given the power from above."

He told them once more: "Peace be with you! As the Father has sent me, I, too, am sending you."

And when he had said that to them, he breathed on them and said to them: "Receive the Holy Spirit.

The Crowning of His Work

Those whose sins you remit shall be forgiven; those whose sins you retain shall be retained by them."

⊕

Thomas, one of the Twelve, called Didymus or the Twin, was not with them when Jesus came. The other disciples told him: "We have seen the Lord!"

But he answered them: "If I do not see in his hands the mark of the nails, if I do not put my finger in the mark of the nails, and if I do not put my hand into his side, I shall not believe any of it!"

Eight days later the disciples found themselves once more in the same room, and Thomas was with them. Jesus entered, though the doors were bolted. He presented himself in their midst and said: "Peace be with you!" Then he said to Thomas: "Put your finger here and look at my hands; stretch forth your hand also and put it into my side; do not be incredulous any more, but believe!"

Thomas exclaimed: "My Lord and my God!"

"Because you have seen me, you have believed!" Jesus told him. "Happy are those who have not seen and who have believed!"

⊕

Later, by the shore of the sea of Tiberias, Jesus manifested himself again to the disciples, in this way:

Simon Peter, Thomas called the Twin, Nathaniel from Cana in Galilee, the sons of Zebedee, and two others of his disciples were assembled. "I am going to fish," Peter told them.

The others replied: "We are going with you."

THE CROWNING OF HIS WORK

They left and climbed into the boat. That night they caught nothing.

When morning came, Jesus was there, standing on the shore. The disciples, however, did not know that it was Jesus. "Children," said Jesus, "do you have anything to eat?" "No!" "Cast the net to the right of the boat, you will find something!" said he.

They cast it, and they did not have enough strength to pull it in, it was so full of fish.

Once they had landed, they saw a brazier prepared with fish on it and some bread. Jesus told them: "Bring a few of the fish that you have just caught."

Simon Peter then climbed into the boat and drew the net onto the land. It was full of big fish; there were one hundred and fifty three, and in spite of this great number the net did not tear. "Come and eat," said Jesus to the disciples. None of them dared to ask him this question: "Who are you?" They knew that it was the Lord. Jesus, approaching, took the bread and gave it to them, as well as the fish.

This was the third time since his resurrection from the dead that Jesus manifested himself to his disciples.

⊕

After the meal, Jesus asked Simon-Peter: "Simon, son of John, do you love me more than these people?" He answered: "Yes, Lord, you know that I love you." Jesus told him: "Tend my lambs."

Then he continued: "Simon, son of John, do you love me?" Again he answered: "Yes, Lord, you know that I love you." "Be the pastor of my ewes," said Jesus.

And for the third time he repeated: "Simon, son of

The Crowning of His Work

John, do you love me?" Peter was saddened at what he was asking him for the third time: "Do you love me?" He answered: "Lord, you know all things, you know that I love you!" Jesus told him: "Put my sheep to pasture! Verily, verily I declare unto you, when you were young, you would gird your loins yourself and went where you wanted to; but when you become old, you will stretch out your hands, another will gird you up and will lead you where you would not want to go."

He expressed himself in this way to indicate by what kind of death Peter was to glorify God.

After having spoken, Jesus added: "Follow me!"

Peter, turning around, saw coming behind him the disciple whom Jesus loved, the one who during the meal had leaned forward and had said to him: Lord, who will betray you? Upon seeing him, Peter questioned Jesus: "Lord, what will happen to this one?" "If I want him to remain until I come," retorted Jesus, "what does it matter to you? You, follow me!"

The rumor spread therefore among the brethren that this disciple would not die. Yet Jesus had not said to Peter: "He will not die," but: "If I want him to remain until I come, what does it matter to you?"

It is this disciple who here bears witness to these things; he himself recorded them in writing; and we know that he is a reliable witness.

⊕

However, the eleven disciples went forth into Galilee, on the mountain to which Jesus had ordered them to go. When they saw him, they bowed down before him. But some doubted. Then Jesus, approaching, spoke to

THE CROWNING OF HIS WORK

them, saying: "All power has been given to me in heaven and on earth. Go, teach all nations, baptize them in the name of the Father, and of the Son, and of the Holy Spirit; teach them to keep everything that I have commanded you. See, I am with you every day, until the end of the world."

⊕

After his passion, Jesus had shown himself alive to his apostles. He had given them numerous proofs of his resurrection, had appeared to them for forty days and had spoken to them concerning the kingdom of God.

One day when he had joined them, he commanded that they do not go away from Jerusalem, but wait there for what the Father had promised: "Which is what I have announced to you," said he; "for John baptized with water, but you, in a few days, will be baptized with the Holy Spirit."

The apostles, even as they were accompanying him, were questioning him: "Lord," they asked, "is it now that you are going to restore the royalty of Israel?" He answered: "It is not for you to know the times or the moments the Father has determined on his own authority. But you will receive the power of the Holy Spirit, which will come down upon you, and you will be my witnesses in Jerusalem, in the whole of Judea, in Samaria, even unto the ends of the earth."

Then he led them as far as Bethany, and, raising his hands, he blessed them. While he was blessing them, he took his leave of them. He was taken up to heaven in their presence, and a cloud came to conceal him from their sight.

The Crowning of His Work

As their eyes were fixed on the heavens while he was moving away, two men dressed in white appeared to them and said: "Men of Galilee, why do you tarry to look at the heavens? This Jesus, who has been taken up to the heavens from your midst, will return from there in the same way as you have seen him going up."

Then, filled with joy, the apostles returned to Jerusalem, from the mountain called the Mount of Olives, which is very close to the town, at the distance of a sabbath walk (about a thousand steps).

Now Jesus did many other signs in the presence of the disciples, which are not written in this book. But these are written so that you may come to believe that Jesus is the Messiah, the Son of God, and that through believing you may have life in is name.[1]

---

[1] Matt. 26:30–35; Mark 14:26–31; Luke 22:31–38; John 13:37–38—Matt. 26:36–46; Mark 14:32–42; Luke 22:39–46—Matt. 26:47–56; Mark 14:43–52; Luke 22:47–54; John 18:1–11—Matt. 26:57–68; Mark 14:53–65; Luke 22:66–71; John 18:12–14, 19–24—Matt. 26:69–75; Mark 14:66–72; Luke 22:55–62; John 18:15–18, 25–27—Matt. 27:1–2, 11–26;2:11–26; Mark 15:1–15; Luke 23:1–7, 13–25; John 18:28–40; John 19:4–16; Luke 23:8–12; Matt. 27:3–10; cf. Acts 1:18–19; Matt. 27:27–30; Mark 15:16–19; Luke 22:63–65; John 19:1–3; Matt. 27:31–32; Mark 15:20–21; Luke 23:26–32; Matt. 27:33–54; Mark 15:22–39; Luke 23:33–47; John 19:17–37; Matt. 27:55–56; Mark 15:40–41; Luke 23:48–49; Matt. 27:57–61; Mark 15:42–47; Luke 23:50–66; John 19:38–42; Matt. 27:62–66; Matt. 28:1–10; Mark 16:1–14; Luke 24:1–11; John 20:1–18; Luke 24:13–33; Matt. 28:11–15; Matt. 28:16–20; Mark 16:14–20; Luke 24:36–49; John 20:19–23; John 19:24–29; John 21:1–14; John 21:15–24; Luke 24:50–53; Acts 1:3–11; John 20:30–31; John 21:25.

THE CROWNING OF HIS WORK

Redemption

EACH HUMAN BEING BURNS FROM THE INNER FIRE OF the self—an ardent, avid fire that consumes everything it can reach. It is beyond our power to destroy this fire, since it is our very being. Only another hand, way above ours, can grasp it and transmute it into light. Nothing stronger than this fire exists—other than in human beings—besides certain gods, the devil, and Jesus. The gods live as we do, by and through their self; the devil seeks only to increase our selfishness. Therefore, God alone can regenerate us.

But between God and us there is the bottomless abyss that separates the infinite from the finite. God, being God, dwelling in his kingdom as such, could reach us only through gestures from above, transmitted and refracted from layer to layer of the relative state. God has to reach us, such as we are, on our own level. So, he will make himself identical to us, embodied as a perfect human being strolling among the multitudes. In this manner, he becomes accessible to our eyes, to our affection, and to our comprehension. Due to the purity of his human embodiment, allowing the presence of his divinity to be incorporated, it follows that all the acts of the man Jesus Christ, the Son of Man, doubtless perfect but human (meaning limited), will receive from the cohabitation of the Word-Son of God limitless radiation, infinite force, and all-powerful momentous worth.

The formulas expressing and conveying this transposition of the measurable with the incommensurable are to be found in the Scriptures and the liturgy: Jesus atoned for our sins; Jesus has redeemed us from our slavery at the price of his blood; he acquitted our debt upon Calvary; he has satisfied justice by means of the immolation of his mercifulness.

The Crowning of His Work

What rendered the terrible drama of the incarnation of the Word necessary was the spark of freedom that the Father deposited within us at the same time as the seed of necessity. From this seed grew our immortal self; from that spark will our eternal soul blossom out. In the parlance of the Real, nothing has any value unless it is done freely, spontaneously. Hence, God interdicted himself from saving us in spite of ourselves. To be saved, we have to want it. But, having been swept along in the avalanche monstrously accrued by our self-appetites, how could we see anything but this avalanche; how could we recall the uncreated spark buried in the depths of the mass of our depredations? This is the reason why the awesome light whence the spark had to descend had to embody itself into a human person, had to reascend laden with this load back to its point of departure, after having caused all the almost extinguished sparks found in the core of each human spirit to flicker up, awakening them out of their lethargy, jolting with a stealthy shudder this mass of substances and forces geared, until then, solely towards their own growth.

Jesus, the innocent, suffered unto death to satisfy justice in our stead, because our sufferings would not have sufficed for acquittal. In fact, our sins are disobediences to God: their worth, their dynamism, becomes infinite because of the infinite grandeur of the One whom they offend. Our sufferings, *per se*, belong to the relative states; no matter how intense they might be, they will never reach the Absolute. Hence, it is the Absolute that must intervene; this intervention is the redeeming Word. This is how things are, seen from the point of view of *justice*.

But there is also the point of view of *love*. It is obvious that intelligence is totally inadequate. In fact, one perceives

THE CROWNING OF HIS WORK

a conflict between the justice of the Father and his benevolence, which Christ would have the mission to reconcile; and if mercy intercedes, it means that justice plays the foremost role in the drama of redemption.

Let us consider that Christ incarnated for our salvation. Once incarnated, he had to amass a treasure of merits with which to pay our debts. At the same time as he was canceling these debts as to quantity through his love, he was wiping them out as to quality. Redemption is the re-ascent, the reconstruction, the transfiguration of this descent, of this destruction, and of this disfigurement which is the natural course of the human species throughout the worlds.

Even before Creation, God conceived through his Word the whole of humanity, deciding we would be his children and that, through this Word, our sins could be erased, so that we personally could be assumed unto heaven. Through the Word, he puts all of his treasures within our grasp; through the Word, he reveals to us his secret design of unifying us all by means of this very same Word, so that union and unity might exist in nature as it is in super-nature. Finally, this self-same Word offers us the eternal legacy, furnishes us with the means of receiving it; and he gives us the comprehension of Verity, which enables us to believe and to receive from the Spirit everything that is within our power to receive from it.

In all of the concrete or abstract, individual or collective, sensible or intelligible, orders during the course of an ordinary earthly life, Jesus is the sole mediator between the relative states and the Absolute. The Word made himself like us, so we could become like him.

Christ, by renouncing his eternal glory and his privileges, causes a new light to flash into the world of the Spirit; he

The Crowning of His Work

applies this light—his merit—to us, thereby making our salvation possible. From then on we can reascend to the Father, through and by the Son. He was our Lord in his very nature; he conquered that seigneury through his incarnation.

Moreover, love alone—i.e., sacrifice alone—permits the transfer of one's own merit to another. To sin is to prefer a created thing to God. To wipe out sin becomes an inverse act of love—which means to love more than one's self, and, to the detriment of self, to love something other than self. As soon as an act has been effected, no one can undo its state of being; no one, except God. Hence the Word is the only One who can erase our sins; he alone can pay our debts in our stead because his treasures alone are inexhaustible, because they alone among all treasures are not the fruits of a deal or a barter.

All of the gifts of the Father to men are comprised, exist, in Christ; in him and through him, the Father grants us mercy; in him and through him, our sins are expunged.

Inasmuch as Christ is God, he could have done it all without egressing from eternity; so why did he compel himself to descend into existence and to death?

So as to give us, to furnish us, the example of a perfect life and of a perfect death; which, having taken place right here on earth, they are closer, more comprehensible to us, and more imitable. Children remember a lesson demonstrated tangibly rather than one acquired and taught from books. And for this example to remain more permanent, more profound and total, Jesus chose the harshest forms of physical life and the most painful death. He always went to the very limit of all things, though he was free to choose the least confines. He always sought the ultimate, so that no man could look at him without finding perfection therein.

THE CROWNING OF HIS WORK

The Garden of Olives

IF ONE HAS THE EXTRAORDINARY CHANCE OF APPROACHing a free man, one often sees him act in a disconcerting manner. He seems to endeavor to provoke mockery, scorn, slander, or suspicion; he does things that the world disapproves of. Thus Jesus, wanting to fulfill the saying: "He was put on a par with malefactors," advises his disciples to equip themselves with supplies, money, and two swords. Was this a simple precautionary measure relative to the penury this small circle was to face during the bewildering days that were to follow? Did he want to draw public censure upon his self? Did he want to offer his executioners the semblance of a pretext? One can answer these three questions affirmatively, yet be quite certain as well that his order of proceeding had been motivated by many other reasons.

This took place, according to the calculations of the most conscientious historians, on the 13th of Nisan of the Roman year 782—otherwise known as the 14th of April of the year 33 of our calendar, at ten o'clock at night. Jesus had the custom of retiring for the night at a place known as Gethsemane (meaning "oil-press"), a spot occupied nowadays by Franciscan monks in whose garden one notices the peculiar flowers called "Passion flowers," born, according to the legend, from the drops of bloody sweat in the shape of which one can recognize the image of the instruments of the Savior's torture. These flowers are the Provençal genus known as *Passi flora*.

The account of this tragic day is so well known that I need not repeat it. The ensemble of these pitiful episodes take on the aspect of the patent junction of two opposite currents, one descending from above, the other rising from

The Crowning of His Work

below. The latter has its source in the icy abode of Lucifer, among those adamantine and immobile landscapes where glitter the dazzling crystals of selfishness. At the source of the former are the infinite vistas of the eternal fields, all-streaming with the fecund light of love. If, as we go through the poignant twists and turns of the drama of the most pathos the earth has ever seen, we keep our eyes fixed upon this dual vision, the meaning of many obscure points will be illuminated by a new, comprehensive, lively light.

All his friends, known and unknown, visible and invisible, earthly as well as celestial, have in fact suffered with him in the same measure as they loved him; as to his enemies, let us ignore them, since he has forgiven them.

Imagine the tragic battle beginning at this moment beneath the vast, star-studded, dark-blue vaulted canopy of heaven, beneath the impassible moon, as perfumes are wafting in this nocturnal coolness through the great eerie silence of the dormant land. The insects and beasts are on the hunt. Against the dark firmament, the adjoining mountains profile their lofty, pearly crests. Like great, tall warriors, the large immobile cypresses stand guard over the tombs and gates of the gardens. The olive trees spread like silvery clouds amid the vigorous grape vines. And in this enchanted decor the most cruel, the most unjust, the most terrifying, struggle is being engaged.

The army of evil rushes up to the tall form seated beneath the shelter of an overhanging rock. Gray vipers and homicidal little scorpions are sliding by without harming this man. But all the demons—the frenzied, violent, cruel ones, the assassins, the insidious, subtle, perverse, morose beings —flock around him, armed with all the forces that all the sinners from the time of Adam had bequeathed to them.

THE CROWNING OF HIS WORK

The spirits of these sins also emerged: the reptilian, the fantastic, the horrific, and glamorous ones; the vampiric chimera of debauchery loosed from the limbos of long-forgotten races; the frozen angels of pride who counseled the universal monarchs; the gods of the satanic initiations and of the infernal sciences; the maharajah's of "what's the use?"; the emperor of the self; the supreme pontiff of immobility. All of them, the least of whom, met face to face, would make us swoon from fear, now emerged together, hitting, torturing, seducing, the very pure human form of the Messiah.

How can we comprehend the terror of such an inmost dissolution? Even our saints have rarely had bouts with any but the weakest of Satan's henchmen; yet what tortures have they not revealed having endured!

Can we imagine these consuming flames shattering the whole physical organism, drying up the flesh to such a degree as to cause the blood of the capillaries to gush out, ruining within an hour or two the whole robustness of this Being, whose organism, pure from any ancestral or personal flaw, already had victoriously withstood unprecedented travails? An entire cohort of tormentors is on its way to take him, but he does not want to die, just yet. That is why, it is said, the angel Gabriel brings him a mysterious beverage to enable him to resist the onslaught of imminent tortures.

Those he loves are asleep; with this fresh wound, he returns beneath the rock. Behold, Satan renews the lures he had offered him when he sallied forth from the desert in the *past*, with all the force, subtlety, and obstinacy that certitude of victory furnishes him. This Being who had driven him away so often, is he not here now, weakened, lonely, lamentable? The infuriated prince of this world persists

The Crowning of His Work

with the enraged certitude of reconquering that heaven whence he had been precipitated.

As defence, Jesus merely presents the shield of these words: "May thy will be done." However, he falters and drags himself towards his disciples, whom he finds asleep. He awakens them for the second time, for fear that the evil one, being so near, may enter into them during sleep.

And he returns to his agony. Now comes the turn of all *future* evil storming his being. All the evil that we have committed, especially we Christians, for the past two thousand years, and all we will commit until the consummation of the world, is there in agile, cruel living forms blasting out as the whirlwind from the granaries of hell. And in silence, Jesus withstands the frightful onslaught, as well as the more treacherous grief that he knows how little his sufferings will serve. We do not fully realize that each of our sins is a real wound that we inflict upon the spirit of the Savior. See how carefully one should tend the humblest demand of life, so as to live it with rectitude!

At this moment, Jesus fears again for his friends, who are still asleep. He awakens them for the third time because the troop of the traitor is approaching the garden's gate. He gives them a few more recommendations, remains standing, and waits. This agony had lasted almost three hours.

Pontius Pilate had loaned Caiaphas five hundred and fifty-five men, who were guarding the various egresses of the path. Hannalus, chief of the pike-men of the temple, was waiting with the centurions at the brook Cedron. People from the police were disseminated here and there. But the Iscariot brought with him only thirty mercenaries and functionaries: all Jews.

I will not repeat the details of the capture of Jesus. Note

only: the fall of the soldiers, a phenomenon similar to the seismic tremors that will occur later at the time of the consummation of the sacrifice; the name of "friend," which Jesus bestows on Judas; and the healing of the servant of the high-priest whom Peter had wounded.

The Tribunals

DURING THE TRAGEDY THAT TERMINATES THE LIFE of the Savior, his heroic method of always choosing the most difficult means manifests itself at every moment. In the Gethsemane garden, he could, by maintaining his divine nature, have avoided suffering from the attacks of the devil. He could have given his disciples the necessary strength not to abandon him. He could have prevented the forthcoming tortures, even death itself; he could have anesthetized his sensibilities. He knew of a thousand means to lessen or annul pain. But to the contrary, all the details of the Passion seem to have been planned, combined, to produce the maximum of physical pangs, moral and spiritual agonies.

The coexistence of the two natures, divine and human, in the sacred person of the Savior is not at all similar to, or of the same order, as the psychical state of the other founders of the great religions. Those beings possessed a strong, even gigantic, personality, very much in advance of the average level of their contemporaries. They were titans as far as their will, their intelligence, and magnetic force are concerned. Moreover, a spiritual entity collaborated with their self in a constant manner. This entity did not descend especially from the Absolute, as it had for Christ (no matter what has been said); it was, might we say, an angel, or one of the gods

The Crowning of His Work

of Creation, united to the will of these superhuman adepts through a sort of mystical marriage, forming thus a sun of attractions and of radiations whose arrows would reach all those men whose personality offered similar structural analogies to theirs.

In our Lord Jesus Christ, on the contrary, the God and the man were one being only. As man, the Man was the purest, the most perfect and most powerful, above any of the other leaders of souls who had come so far; this Man was, in short, the unique instrument, especially forged by the Father—truly, such a being was lofty enough to legitimize by himself our admiration, our love, our respect. The body of Christ, his magnetic and mental fluids, were extracted from the finest essences of nature; merely from their virtue and forces he could have had command over matter, had he wanted to. On the other hand, as I told you long ago, the perfection of his earthly organism was necessary and indispensable, so that he might serve as a suitable medium to the fulgurant divine energies that permeated it.

One can conceive that a few agonies more or less could not frighten a heart whom the gods of the immense ethers tremblingly obey. A few priests, a few soldiers, a few executioners from a small corner of the earth, itself a mere forgotten compartment in the innumerable army of stellar galaxies, could not affect a courage accustomed to the vertigo of the original abysses. Nothing in Jesus's brief and calm responses, or in his silences, could possibly surprise us. He had offered himself freely and consciously to the powers of darkness the night before; hence no torture could astonish him from then on. Condemned in advance, the interrogations of the Roman Pilate, of Herod, and of Caiaphas were but hypocritical formalities.

THE CROWNING OF HIS WORK

However, a few additional incidents can bring some most interesting considerations to mind.

The Passion began on the night of the thirteenth day of Nisan. Hannalus, the chief of the temple's pike-men, who arrested Jesus, was also thirty-three years old, as forty-two years later he would be seventy-five when, following the sacking of Jerusalem, he was arrested, dragged to Rome, and thrown at the feet of the emperor Claudius.

Achazias and Ananias, emissaries of the Sanhedrin, are recognized in the Talmud to be informers in the pay of this august body, with orders to spy upon the doings and activities of Jesus.

Judas, the only Jewish disciple, was born, not from the Moabite Kerioth but from the Karioth situated to the West of Gomorrah near the Dead Sea; and his name may be read, according to the diverse accentuations of the vowel-points as: the leather-belted, the traitor, the man of lies, the usurer, the evil recompense, the hanged man.

Annas was the father-in-law of Caiaphas, the "high-priest that particular year," although the pontificate for life was decreed in the Torah. From the rabbinical standpoint, the sacerdotal acts of Caiaphas and his decisions were worthless. The Nazirite, as sovereign judge, the only one having the power to pronounce a death sentence, had not been summoned. The Levites who were clamoring before Caiaphas had no right to be there. The doctors were deliberately violating the law; the elders, in the pay of Annas, were imposing silence upon Joseph of Arimathea and Nicodemus, although the kabbalist Gamaliel, citing the texts, demanded an open-type defense.

A supernatural feeling of fatality weighed upon everyone. Note how the Talmud reads: "It was during the month of

The Crowning of His Work

Nisan that Israel was freed from Egypt; so will it be freed again during the month of Nisan" (*Rosch Hoschana* 14, 2). Elsewhere, R. Nephtali (*Emech Hammelech* XXXII, 2) writes: "We have a precise tradition which teaches us that redemption will be fulfilled on the eve of the Passover (Easter) as the sabbath begins." And it happens that this particular year was the only one when the month of Nisan contained a Friday that fell on the eve of Easter.

Lastly, Villiers de l'Isle-Adam adds that although the law forbade any kind of domestic fowl to be in Jerusalem (because, living upon manure, they would cause all sorts of insects to fly out that would have corrupted the holocaust meats), yet within the temple's enclosure there was a large solitary rooster, exclusively fed grains by the virgins. This is the bird whose shrill cry announced the four nocturnal watches; the same cock that emphasized Peter's denial. This took place on Friday the 14th of Nisan, at 3 a.m.

The entire responsibility of this heinous offence falls back upon the priests. They avowed it fully as they screamed: "Let his blood fall upon us and upon our children." Their cry was heard, and the downpour they asked for has not stopped yet.

In the texts it is often stated: "Such a thing must take place for the prophecy to be fulfilled." In that case, what happens to free will? Here is what may be said in answer.

God creates, knowing everything it will be possible for creatures to do, what decisions they will make, and what consequences will flow from them—right up to the end of time. He knows this because he forged the hidden springs of all things. From time to time, he indicates to a prophet some details concerning momentous events that will later occur, and this the prophet repeats to those around him. A

THE CROWNING OF HIS WORK

movement is then born among the immediate listeners, which grows and spreads. These listeners find themselves involved in this movement in one or more of their subsequent existences. If their physical memory should fail, it remains nonetheless in their immortal spirits, which work (here as on the other side of the veil) in the direction of the prophecy. In this way, events beneficial to general progress are realized; and the witnesses of the prophecy, who, without knowing it, are also witnesses to the accomplished fact, understand it much better and use it more wisely.

Thus man, in accepting or denying prophecy, calls for or dispels a future providential intervention. According to the adage of astrologers, "an aspect inclines but does not compel."

Hence, Judas's treason and Peter's denial were only probabilities. It is the weakness of our will that cooperates, whether for good or evil, towards the realization of prophecies. The grandeur of the victim also increases the magnitude of the offense. That is why, though the most sordid life is still progress, it would have been preferable for Judas never to have been born; two thousand years of expiation have not yet expunged his crime. Neither has Pilate been redeemed from his pusillanimity; and is not Peter's error the source from which so many scandalous upheavals have sprung?

The only ones who can betray the Master are those whom he has chosen to live beside him. We, to whom a little faith has been given, we too have been chosen by him, and our spirit lives close to his spirit. Although we are still impure and imperfect, we are nevertheless his familiars. Let us be on watch, because, more than other men, we will be tempted to betray him. All sins are treachery. If we do not

The Crowning of His Work

serve him, we oppose him. Jesus sees us and knows us as he knew his apostles. He reads within our hearts. Let us not seek out a host of maxims to sustain us. Let us tell ourselves throughout each day that we are in the real presence of Christ, he who has faith in us and who loves us.

Judas the Iscariot did not become a traitor at the moment Jesus offered him the bread, nor did Satan enter into him at that moment. For months and months, proud of his intelligence, scornful of the other apostles' simpleness, he harbored greeds, envies, and rancors; for a long time he had been inviting the devil, and when the definitive moment of the possession occurred, Jesus had the supreme mercy to deposit into this pitiful heart the seed of salvational repentance.

We must not evince contempt towards Judas the Iscariot, because we commit analogous sins daily; and each sin is a betrayal. As the most cultured among the apostles, and perhaps the most beloved of the Master, has he not, in short, dolorously served towards the salvation of everyone?

Some Western initiations that tie in closely to Rosicrucianism give some rather curious information regarding the Passion. Setting aside the legend according to which Pontius Pilate would have committed suicide in his despair by throwing himself from one of the mountains that bear his name at Lucerne and at Lyons, there are people who assert that he has returned to earth often, leading a restless existence on the very spots wherein the purest manifestations of the spirit of Christ have been taking place.

It is also said that the tree, the branches of which were used to make the crown of thorns, is this thorny tamarisk shrub that grows in the desert. It is the same tree that many centuries before had hidden the corpse of Osiris; it is the same that was planted upon the tomb of Hiram, and with the wood of which the ancient Arabs sculpted the image of their god Al-Uzza, whose cult was abolished by Muhammad. This thorny acacia is the symbol of immortality.

Folklore would reveal many other things just as curious; all of them having but a symbolic archaeological value; but to try to unravel superstitions from facts in this mass of popular beliefs would be a long-winded task.

The Crucifixion

WE ARE NOW APPROACHING THE DENOUEMENT OF THE divine tragedy. The sacrifice that began with the nocturnal tortures, the agony, the betrayal, the flagellation, the insults, the crowning of thorns, will continue with the carrying of the cross, and will consummate its dolorous septenary with the crucifixion.

The seven falls of Jesus—exhausted, famished, bleeding, crushed beneath the heavy load, blinded by the torrid sun, being beaten and jostled by the crowd while climbing up the rugged, stony path—emphasize the phases of the last effort of his redemptive love. The poor people of the Middle Ages, so oppressed and so miserable, communed easily with their God under the form of this episode: the numerous ways of the cross one finds in Catholic countries prove it. Moreover, it is regrettable that the customs of these commemorations have been forsaken, because in these practices lie one of the greatest reserves of the invisible force found within religion.

The earthly bystanders as well as the invisible witnesses to the sacrifice were twofold: the friends and the enemies. And as will shortly be demonstrated, power and material

The Crowning of His Work

success will be on the side of the enemies; the friends merely lament and accept to bear the blows of destiny.

On the crest of Golgotha, very close to the cross, were eighteen friends, including the Virgin and John; while the executioners, mercenaries born in Catalogna, numbered also eighteen.

The cross was in the shape of a Tau, to which a short extension had been added upon which they fastened the signboard of the sentence. When the empress Helena, mother of Constantine, found the cross, it was concluded that the space between the holes bored for the hands proved that Jesus must have been very tall. He was slightly taller than the average, but had long arms; besides which, as the executioners had bored the holes for the hands in advance without taking any measurements, they had violently pulled the wrists of the Lord with cords, almost dislocating his shoulders, so that his palms would reach the places prepared. Only one nail was used for the feet. Once the hoisting of the cross, with all the brutality of the drunken executioners (thereby increasing his already unutterable suffering), was endured, and with the brusque change of position inflicted upon the martyr, the cross found itself oriented in such a way that his august face was turned to the northwest. Thus did Europe receive the last regard of the Savior. According to the tradition of Jerusalem, preserved by the Fathers of the Church, the tree of the mystical press was planted upon the exact spot where the body of Adam lies. In any event, Golgotha signifies "place of the skull." That is why all the religious paintings of the primitives depict a skull at the foot of the cross.

All Jesus had endured for the past fourteen hours would have killed any other man. Although toughened by hardships and sufferings, solely his superhuman vitality and extraordinary athletic constitution were enabling him to withstand the moral and physical tortures that would only end two hours later. Because, to say it once again, the man alone in Jesus Christ endured the Passion; the God in him did not come to his help—all of this, so that we humans could profit from this unique example.

As you know, every man possesses connections, more or less numerous, with the rest of the world, especially with the earth. Within the confines of our spirit (according to its grandeur) lives a host of spirits of subordinate creatures belonging to all of the hierarchies of physical and supra-physical forces. Any event that comes to us, before being able to affect our ordinary consciousness first must pass through inner spaces to each inhabitant of which it will cause some kind of perturbation. When this shock finally reaches the material form of these spiritual beings, a portent follows. Therefore, when you consider a being as gigantic as the Man-God, you will not be surprised for his death to be accompanied by remarkable phenomena such as an eclipse, darkness, earthquakes, and the tearing of the temple's sacred veil, as mentioned in the Bible.

At the moment when the tree of salvation—the trunk of the spiritual vine whose mysterious form upholds the universe—was lifted up, an eclipse of the sun occurred. Needless to mention the alchemical, magical, and theosophical dissertations that adepts have subtly drawn and elaborated on that theme. Many would certainly be found to be sublime, but the simple facts are still more instructive, and speak with a more pressing eloquence. The masonic symbolisms, the spagyric models, the visions of a Jacob Boehme; the paintings of a Pico de la Mirandola, or the

The Crowning of His Work

speculations of a Father Sabbathier, as lofty as they are, still belong to the external. What is internal is always more accessible, when based upon facts; but do note that, in its essence, it is often inexpressible.

The skylark rising from the furrows on the right-hand side of a man walking foretells a happy incident to him; and when we are about to die, the screech-owl announces it from the roof top. So when the corporeal body of the One by whom the whole universe subsists ceases to live, this universe can very well express its confusion by means of an abnormal phenomenon. The moon, the stars, and the sun that have lit successively the phases of this great sacrilege, can very well veil themselves in despair; and the rock that lent itself to the execution of this crime can very well shatter abeam its veins in sheer terror: they are all responsible.

One does not know what forces or beings are the veritable factors of rain, of thunder, or of earthquakes; one does not know who are the marvelous cavaliers for whom comets are the mounts! True meteorology is lost, and astronomy resting simply upon *petitio principii*, is exact only now and then. To him who knows a little about the life of things, there is nothing surprising in the fact that, here and there, navigators around the world heard the spirits of nature wailing: "The great Pan is dead."[2]

---

[2] According to the historian Plutarch, a few decades before his birth (during the reign of Emperor Tiberias, who ruled at the time of Christ), an Egyptian navigator named Thamus, sailing by the Greek islands, heard a divine voice call to him: "The great god Pan is dead!" Writers of the early Christian era spread this story, believing the divine voice to have been that of Christ. In Anne Catherine Emmerich's visions of the life of Christ (on the subject of various apparitions in the wake of the Passion) we read: "I saw a harbor in which lay many ships... I saw there

THE CROWNING OF HIS WORK

Attached to the cross, agonizing from inexpressible death pangs, Jesus uttered several phrases; but only seven were kept. In themselves they form an admirable synthesis of his teachings. The first three ask for mercy for his executioners, for sinners, for his most faithful friends. Forgiveness for those who commit evil in ignorance; hope granted to repentance; the perpetuation of his spiritual presence upon this earth—here were his first three bequests. His fourth saying was the excuse for and the attenuation of all despair to come; just as his fifth was his authorization for us to ask for material help. By saying: "All is consummated," the Messiah substantiates the realization of his ancient promise: "I did not come to destroy but to accomplish." In fact, the Great Work has been accomplished. The light is now being shed everywhere. All the fields have received the seeds. Now it is left up to the created beings to do the rest. As far as the great sower is concerned, he entrusts the forces that served him to fulfill his horrendous mission into the hands of his Father.

Louis-Claude de Saint-Martin was accustomed to say that the number five had to receive permission to exert its control upon the body of Christ, and that it was the reason a fifth wound—the spear-thrust—had to be inflicted upon that innocent victim. If one attempts to probe into what were the invisible effects of the sufferings endured during

---

a man, a pagan, the custodian of the ships, whose duty was to gaze out over the ocean to see whether ships were coming, or were in need of assistance. Hearing a roaring noise among the ships in the harbor, he hurried up into the watchtower and beheld floating over the ships numerous dark figures that cried out to him in mournful tones: "If you desire to save these ships, steer them away from here, for we have to go into the abyss! Great Pan is dead."

The Crowning of His Work

the Passion, one notices that each of them, down to the least, engenders—down to the depths of the spheres and in the far distant future—results that are as extraordinary as they are mysterious. When at the beginning of the eleventh century the anonymous monk of Murbach writes that from the wound of Christ's side flowed all the virtues of the sacraments, he expresses a hidden truth. We must reiterate that everything lives, and that everything transforms itself without disappearing. Were we to know the cosmic origin of each species of cells that the tortures of the Passion killed in the body of the Savior, we could deduce from it which spiritual forces were generated from them into the mystical body of the Christian Church. However, we know that the blood of Jesus, profusely shed, was the physiological expression of the form of the sacrifice that was boiling within his superhuman heart. It is this pure and precious substance, this blood which, sublimated by the very mysterious alchemy of the guardian angel of Christianity, has made it possible for a rather great number of men to realize perfect abnegations.

Do not interpret it to mean that for this one has to adore in the person of the Savior something else than the God. He personally never ceases repeating to us that it is the Father, and the Father alone, whom we should invoke and address in prayer. However, it is preferable to render a cult to the Sacred Heart, and to invoke a saint, than not to pray at all.

The drawing of lots for the clothing of Jesus Christ is still one of those mysterious but frequent circumstances in his life that appear in the eyes of the disciple as infinitely fecund seedings of future important events. The Word, in fact, is always veiled to us. No one has yet been permitted to contemplate his ineffable essence. Even the purest mystics have only caught sight of him enveloped within a more or less radiant body. No man could subsist before the insupportable glare he radiates within his own abode. Therefore, religions are but images external to him, images that are more or less exact, accurate, as well as more or less tarnished. Christianity, which in its complete form is still the best among religions, is the seamless robe—whole and immutable. If Christianity were to change, it would not be itself. And the four other lots that the soldiers claimed and divided among themselves are the four great religions prevailing on earth.

Resurrection

WHILE HIS BODY WAS REPOSING IN THE SEPULCHER, Jesus descended, according to the prevailing—and veridical—tradition of the Church, into the subterranean limbos where the souls of the just of ancient times and of righteous pagans were pining for him. It would not be right to believe that these ancients had been, ever since their death, enclosed in a special place. According to the Hebraic doctrine (very close on that point to that of the Brahmans), one reincarnated within the religious and social sphere one belonged to until all the civic and religious precepts of that sphere had been totally fulfilled. Then one went on for a period of rest to one of the heavens or paradises that formed the superior planes of that said egregore.[3] But these paradises were not beatific, since the dispenser of beati-

---

[3] *Egregore*: an invisible yet tangible spirit form of a state of being. The embodiment of a "whole."

The Crowning of His Work

tudes—the Word—had not yet manifested himself therein. It is only on this particular day and this one night, commemorated as Holy Saturday, that the just, led by the spirit of Christ, were able to leave the fluidic orbit of the earth definitively.

Besides which, for the last time, Jesus traversed certain regions of these sub-physical realms that contained the centers or foci of radiant energies, the existence of which gave birth to the false concept of a geocentric hell. Diverse human and nonhuman races of beings inhabit these regions, whose body, intelligence, and senses are dissimilar from those who people the surface of the globe. Among these are found some pious, some atheistic, some violent, some peaceful, some dwarfish, and some giant races; they have arts, rudimentary sciences, and religious notions; they are generally laggards, benighted. Jesus had visited them all diverse times during his earthly sojourn.

Certain seers, notably Anne Catherine Emmerich,[4] have described this last inspection as the imprisonment of the devils and of Lucifer, which have been fettered from that time until 1940, when heaven will release them for a temporary freedom in order that they may take part in the great battle of the Antichrist which must precede the reign of God on earth. At the death of Jesus Christ certain infernal hierarchies had been immobilized, but they were not among those inhabiting the center of the globe. Just before the advent of the twentieth century, they were given permission to come back here, little by little. These nefarious visitors are going to swarm as time goes on.

---

[4] Anne Catherine Emmerich (1774–1824), German seeress (especially of the life of Christ) and stigmatic.

THE CROWNING OF HIS WORK

At present we are concerned with one of the circumstances discussed among exegetes, rationalistic critics, and the adversaries of the gospel thesis. They have invented all sorts of theories to destroy the Christian precept of the real death of Christ, of his burial, and of his resurrection. Adepts of a false esotericism have explained how this death was merely lethargic and that the resurrection was no more than a sort of magical sleight-of-hand or spirit-like legerdemain. However that might be, one cannot in any case combat their arguments upon the terrain of reason, any more than it is possible to prove the divinity of Jesus. These truths which the Church claims belong to the domain of faith arise from the divine order. Those who accept and admit this to be true are those who have done good, who have lived honorably for such a long time that it enables the illumination of grace to pour into them.

The Christic tradition hands down to us that Jesus really died on the cross; that his body was really deposited in a new sepulcher—but that this body (none of the cells of which was of earthly origin) could not be kept by the spirit of the earth, which had no right to it; that this body within three hours returned, by a sort of disintegration (of which perhaps certain spiritistic phenomena may give some idea) to the heavenly body from which its elements came; and that this work was effected by a cohort of superhuman invisible beings, the chiefs of whom were the two angels seen by the holy women upon arriving at the tomb the next morning. These were the same friends who furnished Christ the semi-material elements necessary to make his double visible and tangible for the twelve apparitions that occurred during the forty-day interval between his death and his ascension.

The Crowning of His Work

Saint Theresa of Avila says that the first visit of the resurrected Christ was not to the holy women but to the Virgin. This is a tradition peculiar to Spain. In the past, on Easter morning, in certain cities of that country, they carried the statue of Mary in a procession, which they would cause to meet with another procession with the Host, at sunrise. The old theologians, St Hilaire, Rupert, abbot of Deutz (twelfth century), St Isidore of Seville, Amalaire Fortunatus, Raban Maur, affirm that the resurrection took place on a Sunday; that Saturday, the day of Saturn, naturally corresponds to the passage of Christ in the lower worlds; and that the sabbath, being therefore overridden, the marvelous miracle *par excellence* was henceforth to mark the beginning of the week. For an analogous reason, the color white has been chosen as that of the Pascal liturgy.

Jesus forbids Magdalene to touch him ("I have not yet ascended to my Father") because of the violent intensity of his love; also because the corporeal appearance he had assumed was too radiant, too subtle, as is proven by the suddenness of his apparitions and of his disappearances at Emmaus, in the cenacle (upper-room), on the lake of Tiberias, and other places.

Theology teaches that the resurrected body of Christ possessed the qualities of glorious bodies, to wit: beauty, perfect health, distinctness, incorruptibility; limpidity; light (the property of emitting some sort of visible aura); agility (which depicts the suppression of effort and of distance); and impassibility (the power of being insensible to external agents, and of being invulnerable).

However, the corporeal substance of the Savior was something other than this; it consisted of a mixture of his double with a particular matter brought from the sun by these "angels," two of whom had permitted themselves to be seen seated upon the stone of the sepulcher by the disconsolate Magdalene. Our body, at the last resurrection, the veritable body of glory, will be differently composed.

The Apparitions

JESUS IMPARTED THE HOLY SPIRIT WHEN HE PAID HIS first visit to the disciples in his resurrected body. For this effusion to be possible, he had to have totally terminated his work on earth, because the Spirit does not precede, but follows him; because the Holy Spirit connects him perpetually to the Father, the Consoler never comes into any locale until the Word has left it physically.

Jesus gave the apostles their mission: to go out into the world as he himself had gone out into it. Indeed, they would go nowhere unless he himself had gone out to sow the seeds. So he gives them the Holy Spirit the first time, which enables them to remit sins, which means to effect healings. The second time, they receive the Consoler, who will confer intelligence upon them. In reality, this divine breath disaggregates within us the shells of matter and of the self, owing to which we are limited to perceiving objects merely as they appear to be and in their relationships with us. The apostles' memory became vivified. They recalled the teachings of their Master and understood most of them. They understood some of the secrets of nature. They began to comprehend universal life, with its innumerable modifications within stones, plants, animals, man, and invisible created beings.

We do not know—no created being can know—what the Holy Spirit is. At best we can barely perceive what he is

The Crowning of His Work

not. Hence, it is impossible to explain the mechanism of his operation. Let us be satisfied, then, with ascertaining its effects. Here again, the simplest image we form is still the one that will inform us best. The Spirit is the antithesis of matter: their characteristics and virtues are opposites. Thus, matter engenders ignorance and evil, whereas the Spirit engenders knowledge and purification.

And so, when one has received the Consoler, one can know the truth of all things; one can transmute the evil within any creature into good—not *chase away* evil (which is but a shift of residence), but *convert* evil, thereby enabling vices to become virtues and diseases to become strengths.

But if such a man at any given time changes direction, beginning to give in to the self once more and no longer living in God, the Spirit takes wing and the powers that man had received volatize. Throughout the history of religions in Europe, one can follow proofs of this statement.

To the Israelite, to remit sins meant to suspend divine anger in such a way that the delinquent would have nothing but the consequences of his faults to pay for—that is, as far as they concerned him, as well as the beings that had had to bear an ensuing prejudice. But the true Christian believes that God does not get angry (contrary to what too many religious ministers affirm today). Remission of sins then becomes the cleansing, the removal, of the stain and of its consequences. The penitent becomes pure. He may start upon a new life. But let him beware of falling again, for a second fall would be worse than the first. This is one of the reasons it is preferable to suffer our woes in patience, because all along the course of such testing, forces are being tempered within us that will permit us, at a later date, to

THE CROWNING OF HIS WORK

resist successfully. This is also why heaven rarely intervenes directly in the march of the world.

Let us bear illness, poverty, and sorrow with the sentiment that we have deserved these tribulations—one must always pay one's debts. And let us rest assured that if we do not meet the angel who would release us with a word, it means we are not yet strong enough to conquer this battle against the self, which is always the price exacted for favors from heaven.

The episode of Thomas's incredulity shows us once more how limited are the ordinary capacities of our mentality, how we circumscribe our own points of view with our narrow-mindedness. The domain of faith is solely supernatural. By definition it extends beyond our intelligence, our comprehension, and our conscience. It is even above the concepts that exceptional beings such as adepts of esotericism or clairvoyants can discern. Nothing the universes can engender pertains to the order of fideistic truths because all this may be perceived at a certain stage of the development of our sensibility, of our intelligence, and of our will.

Christ enters, in spite of closed doors, to confer peace upon the assembly. The scene of persuading the doubter Thomas unfolds. Christ says: "Happy are those who have not seen but who believe." And the narrator relates this episode "so that you too may believe."

This fifth apparition clearly elucidates the one intended for the intellect as well as for this apostle of the East, where everything is taught in keys of five. As his name indicates,[5] Thomas possesses within himself the twofold mystery, the twin of intelligence and faith. Precursor to the "angel of the

---

[5] The name Thomas signifies "twin."

The Crowning of His Work

schools" (St Thomas Aquinas), he brings the light to the lands that became the initiators of the pagan world. He was the first, ancient "angel of the schools," the echoes of which became the fountainhead to Aristotle's science.

Will this episode, in which everything implies the problem of certitude, become sensate, or fideistic? The reasonable answer would be that Jesus, being so well known to Thomas, would have left him in his state of incredulity. But no, Jesus pities him, loves him, wants to give him a proof, since faith had not yet been born in him. Thus are all doubters and uncompromising rationalists forgiven in advance. The tenderness of Jesus, then, authorizes us to make use of our physical, mental, and soul senses. It is the twin who is the actor in this scene, because in our soul twins are born as soon as the soul enters into earthly existence: the sense of the world both visible and invisible, abstract and concrete; and the sense of the divine, of the Uncreated.

Faith, then, demands absolute inflexibility: on one hand, this inflexibility applies solely to the unique fact of the real divinity of Jesus Christ; on the other, it must be maintained within our own self so as to express itself solely by means of a concise declaration, especially through actions and by never forcing anyone to accept it, or by trying to convince them.

You who do not possess this unshakable, unflinching faith; you who still need to understand; you who fear missing proofs—exert your energies to that end!

⊕

Matters relating to faith are acceptable only when one transcends common sense, the rational, and the probable. That is how one must understand the adage: *Credo quia absurdum* (I believe because it is absurd). And the leitmotif of the union of science and faith that has become banal these days is one of those short-sighted views in which the self-complacency of modern intellectualism wallows, because what the Church proffers as being mysteries is generally misinterpreted by the semi-intuitives who swarm in our time. Our most astute thinkers interpret these dogmas as ontological, sociological, or psychological symbols; but the phenomena in which one recognizes the Trinitarian rule are no other than prolongations of the dogma of the Trinity. When some fiction writer who in his youth received a tincture of esotericism spews out dithyrambic verses upon the symbolism of the Virgin Mother, or upon the Incarnation of the Word, he mistakes the shadows for reality. He has no idea of what the Virgin and the Word are: these entities belong to the realm of faith. He could receive the intuition thereof only upon renouncing *in toto* his painfully acquired science, his whole intellectual culture, and all his personal mental categories.

That is why, when one wants to be reborn in the divine, one must have experienced death both in a natural sense and in an inwardly human sense. The ancient initiations were aware of this within their sphere, and were putting it into practice, which is something modern seekers would do well to remember.

For instance, to remit sin, drive out demons, understand the language of nature, drive serpents away, be immune to poisons, heal the sick, and teach the word of God—such are the seven privileges of the apostles in their function as soldiers of heaven. I say privileges, because these are extraordinary faculties, and from the standpoint of justice are

The Crowning of His Work

unmerited. The tiniest spark from the Absolute is, in fact, worth more than all the marvels in the world, since that spark would suffice to give birth to all of them; whereas, through his own efforts, the most perfect man would never be able to obtain them. Besides which, these favors are not the common lot. The greatest saints remained unknown, living a life in the shadows, which never caught the attention of the crowds. The goal in life is not to accomplish miracles, but to follow the Master's example step by step. Moreover, he guides men of goodwill with a most precise solicitude. The true disciple will not seek ecstasies, but will instead consider them as adjunct or accidental encouragements. And if miracles come in response to his prayers, he will plunge more deeply into humility and preserve his anonymity. In short, no matter how exalted a guide may be, he may lead us astray. Christ alone is infallible. It is up to us to prepare our hearts, that we may understand his counsels and his orders.

We can say very little regarding the Ascension. Technically, one explains it as the very natural consequence of the particular quality of the resurrection body. There are substances upon which the terrestrial center of gravity has no effect; their attracting force lies elsewhere, for everything in nature is attracted somewhere.

St Bonaventure and Denys the Carthusian claim that this last prodigy took place on Mount Tabor, which might also have been the site, or theater, for the Transfiguration. Regarding this event, the ancient ecclesiastical chroniclers relate that when St Helena, mother of Constantine, wanted to erect a basilica upon that mountain, the workmen were unable to pave the spot where, it was claimed, the Savior's feet had stood, or to enclose the building's dome.

THE CROWNING OF HIS WORK

As to the moral developments that the Ascension may suggest, you will find a great many in books on Catholic mysticism.

The Future

WHAT IS MOST CONSOLING AND PRECIOUS IS THE PROmise Jesus made to his disciples—that he would always be with them until the end of the world. One can interpret this presence in several ways.

First, it is a remembrance, a recollection, a mental or psychic influence similar to the one by which the work of a man of genius, such as Plato or Dante, is still radiating centuries after the death of its author. In that sense, Jesus would have simply indicated that men would remember him, his words, and his works until the end of the world, and that a good number among them would thereby modify their conduct and their convictions.

Besides which, theologians teach that Jesus has left in the hearts of all men of goodwill, even the idolaters (especially within the circle of Christianity and more particularly in the Roman Church), an active spiritual influence on earth by means of which is perpetuated: the power of sacramental words, of rites; the inspiration within Councils; the inspiration of popes; the sanctity of the faithful; and the general progress of civilization. You will find the development of this thesis in the philosophical histories of Christianity, such as in those of Chateaubriand, Montalembert, Alexandre Vinet, Ozanam, and many others. All of this does not go beyond the bounds of what is rational, probable, or of ordinary intuition.

Since his departure, the promise made by Christ has

The Crowning of His Work

received temporary confirmation—very living and real—within small groups of unknown friends. It is affirmed among them that the Word manifests himself physically, under the cover of some anonymous personage whose real identity lets itself be perceived only by some rare disciples. If everything is possible to the imagination of a mystic, everything is far easier for God. Nothing can invalidate such a claim, such an opinion; nothing can prove it. It belongs to the order of concepts that are beyond the most subtle intelligence, beyond the most audacious psychic experience.

On the other hand, the last conversations that Christ had with Peter and John may serve as themes to quite a few controversies upon the legitimacy of the sacerdotal institution. Actually, neither you nor I have to take sides in the dispute between Rome and Geneva. It suffices that something exists, for us to accept it, since nothing happens without divine permission, and there is some good to be found in everything.

Regarding this matter, remember that in all religions an *outer* as well as an *inner* hierarchy coexist. Indeed, you will find this in the model of the constitution of the human being as offered in China, India, ancient Judaism, and Islam. Indeed, these two hierarchies have always coexisted in Christianity also, especially in Catholicism. But, as we ourselves belong to this system, it can be somewhat challenging for us to understand its functioning. It is sufficient to consult one or another sufficiently complete history of the Church to notice how many times the pope or sacred college have obeyed some secret pressure in the administrative domain.

Moreover, the fact is that there is another twofold set of hierarchies in all religions: the exoteric and the esoteric, the visible and the hidden. The former belongs to the chief of the apostles; the second is affiliated with John. It is still more remarkable that all of the Johannine sects—the Gnostics, Templars, Albigenses, the misguided mystics of all nuances who went to war against Rome in the name of tradition, of occultism, or of the gospel—have almost always erroneously misunderstood this very gospel they profess to defend; and because of this, have nothing in common with the unknown chain of the authentic disciples of Christ, carefully recruited by him and taught inwardly by his spirit.

Were we only considering the number of vanity-stricken simpletons, charlatans, maniacs, and unhinged dupes who follow the banner of occult sciences today, we would easily agree with the Church that proscribed its study. In short, one finds a mixture of the spirit of malice and the spirit of wisdom in esotericism as in exotericism.

If the external sacerdotal ministry, or priesthood, is twofold, then, besides dissidents linked more or less with ancient traditions, there have always been true disciples, taught directly by heaven, who remained in the shadows, excluded from fame, according to the saying: "The world knows you not." These are the direct successors of John the Virgin, and not of these "Johannite" amateurs of polychromatic syncretisms, where odds and ends of Mazdaism, Thebain fragments, reminiscences of the Kabbalah, Sufi intuitions, and Buddhistic news-mongering are jumbled together, cobbling mock mosaics out of symbolic interpretations of the gospel.

As to the common tradition in the Greek Church that John never died, it is refuted by the majority of Catholic theologians. However, it is to be noted nonetheless that not the least authentic relic of the Seer of Patmos exists. The

The Crowning of His Work

Christians of Lebanon possess (if I remember rightly) a similar legend concerning St George and El Khadir; the kabbalists held the same belief regarding Enoch and Elijah. There is a remarkable, little-known mystery in this, which we will attempt to clarify.[6]

Any created being is the materialization, the natural expression, of a spiritual force—of an Idea, as Plato would say. Through births, lives, and deaths, this creature passes ceaselessly through the triple phases of formation, de-formation, and transformation. On earth, for instance, the spirit of this created being has need from one life to another (in order to reorganize the fluidic elements for its new body) of a material point of support. The Kabbalah refers to this when it states that in the corpse one tiny bone always remains intact, serving as the pole of attraction for the fluidic elements and microscopic cells with which a new body is built for the new existence of the deceased.

Apply this now to a vaster being, to the collective spirit of a religion for example: from the beginning to the end of its evolution, its visible body would contain one cell on permanent guard serving as rallying point, pivot, and center of biological gravity. And John, the "son of thunder," the only apostle having remained outside the circle of generative attractions, who had merited being the adoptive son of the Virgin, seems to have assembled all the necessary virtues for this role of immutable witness to the Master, and of "pole" for his true Church.

From the time of the genuine communities of primitive Christianity, a small group of secret friends of the Lord has

---

[6] See also Honore-Victor Guerin, *Description de l'Île de Patmos et de l'Île de Samos* (Paris: Editions Auguste Durand, 1856).

THE CROWNING OF HIS WORK

perpetuated itself. First in Italy, then in France, in Switzerland, in Flanders, in Spain, and back again to Italy and France. These unknown friends, outside of any religion, have felt the presence of, have known, a close relationship with the Spirit of Truth.

While respecting the secret of such a blessing, one may say that the Spirit of Truth, this divine Being, has never ceased and never ceases to sustain, in the mystery of orison, an incessant fight against the most diverse, subtle forms of error. He never rests, never closes his eyes, never falters. Because he fights with the sole sword of meekness, with the sole shield of pardon, he seems always to be the vanquished: he, the vanquisher *par excellence*!

He knows his faithful, having followed them step by step from the distant past, having even witnessed their coming down from heaven. During numerous cycles he has guided them, day by day, month after month. He has nursed and nourished them. He has borne their prayers up to the throne of God and applied celestial balms to their wounds.

He follows the march of the world better than the Rosicrucians or the adepts of the White Lodge Brotherhood. He supervises the progress of civilization, the descent of sciences, the cultivation of fraternity. Being unfailingly accessible to the humble and to the weak, the proud and the powerful ignore him, or else keep searching for him in vain. He remains, as it is written, with the friends of our Lord Jesus Christ. He lives in and within them, through the light. He is the aspect under which the Word has promised to remain among us. And the whole gospel, the entire teachings of Christ, embrace all the methods of joining him.

The Crowning of His Work

Recapitulation

LET US NOW CAST A BACKWARD GLANCE UPON THE course we have pursued together. We find it to be the history of a divine being, starting out in abject and miserable temporal feebleness to arrive, through an uninterrupted ascension, up to the greatest spiritual power. His life is the dual antithesis of the life of *political* power personified by the Roman Caesars, and the life of *intellectual* power personified by Apollonius of Tyana (whom so many ignorant theorists consider an equal of the Master of Nazareth).

Thus, the world always moves on in ternaries: at every moment of its evolution, the fateful wrongdoers (products of antecedent causes), the efforts of humankind to seize the reins of supremacy, and the divine help offered it as providential envoys, can be distinguished in its state.

The gospel is the story that retraces the mission of one of these—the greatest, the purest, the most sublime, and the one within the reach of us all. This light, the most resplendent the earth has ever seen shining, rapidly grows from an imperceptible spark to the fulguration of a sun that will soon glow from one extremity of the world to the other.

The birth of Jesus, his life as a man, his teaching, his miracles, his redemption, his Passion, and his ascension constitute the seven phases of an unparalleled drama that offers to the seeker a vast initiation-canvas—a panorama more complete than the crypts of India, sanctuaries of Thebes, and monasteries of Tibet were ever able to offer their neophytes. One must have fathomed these ancient theophanies to the very end to dare, without presumptuousness, to compare them with a book as simple (on the face of it) in appearance as the teachings of the gospel, and so at odds with what human wisdom has always taught. Unless you remain for many years in the theoretical and practical study of ancient esotericism, you will have to exert such violence upon your self, that barely one among a hundred thousand would be capable of placing himself in the inner state indispensable for perceiving the gospel light; but no matter how painful this second method might be, it is far preferable to the first.

Once this heroic effort has been accomplished (the gospel refers to it simply as "repentance"), examine the limpid verses from all sides, from diverse viewpoints, from all angles—and little by little you will recognize its depth and evidence. Therein you will find all the knowledge, the science, of the world, of man, and of God. The secret wisdom of the ancients hidden in the gospels is far more profound than what adepts ever knew: the true science of numbers, wonders, signatures, initiation, aesthetics, sociology, and philosophical music—all are there indicated for those who know how to read according to their proper methods, that is, who make use of the great secret of their mastery, which is no other than moral development.

The initiates who elaborated the ritualistic forms of Christianity have constructed an admirable ceremonial monument that to the eye of the connoisseur appears as a masterpiece far more perfect than that of the ancient Brahmans. The initiates have employed the same twelvefold plan, known from antediluvian times under the form of the zodiac. Christ is the center; each of the twelve apostles is a sign; each of the seven sacraments is a planet; the former are the boundaries of the monad, the latter its centers of reintegration. Christmas and the feast of St John are the two poles; Lent, Easter, Ascension, Pentecost, and All

The Crowning of His Work

Saint's Day retain an instructive correspondence with the zodiacal signs in which they occur. So that on this circumference, regularly divided by the Father, the Son, and the Holy Spirit (to which the respective practices of faith, charity, and hope lead), the earthly life of Christ from Christmas to Easter occupies three and a half signs of the zodiac, a number that one knows plays an important role in Hindu texts and among the Jewish prophets.

The liturgical year remains a masterpiece of symbolism. Whether one studies its chronological divisions, its settings, or its formulas, it offers the researcher a mine of observations and discoveries that has hardly begun to be explored. We still know nothing regarding the "Kabbalah" of Latin; we have never really broached the hidden virtues of plainchant; we have barely correlated and compared a few architectural numbers and symbols found in stones and windows of stained glass; we have never perceived that the ensemble of the ceremonies of the Mass retrace the whole cosmic drama, the entire heroic saga of regeneration; within the sacraments, we have merely discerned the letter, or at most the moral symbolism. Within this field lies enough work for a cohort of scholars and esotericists to delve into.

In a word, everything is contained in the gospel. In it, one finds all the wisdom of the Vedas, Upanishads, Kings, Avesta, Zohar, and Koran. Nowhere else in our solar system (even were there to be found therein dazzling civilizations next to which ours would seem barbarous) does there exist a book more replete with science and the mysteries than is the gospel.

But thanks to the admirable elasticity of the Spirit that fills its pages, this book alone keeps its secrets, revealing them only to those who melt, as it were, with all their heart

THE CROWNING OF HIS WORK

and soul, into the Being of Light who is its true author. It is because the gospel doesn't require long study or arduous journeys to master, and so lies within everyone's reach, that scholars, philosophers, and esotericists know so little about it, and generally hold it in low esteem.

It is time to do something about this! It would be a worthy attempt, and I hope it will soon be taken up. For such a task, however, philology and exegesis are useless. Only purity of heart and humility can bring us enlightenment. Modernists, expecting results from science that it is incapable of providing, mistake shadow for reality, and embark on a false path.

The text of the gospel as we have it is not the pristine, original text. As St John gives us to understand in his last chapter, this text was voluminous: certain words or sentences of Christ have been deleted or suppressed, others falsified by unscrupulous politicians; many authentic stories (I do not refer to the Apocrypha) have been expunged; certain dates have been arranged according to the symbolistic needs of Alexandrians imbued with the mysteries of Egypt, so that in the end we have an ensemble that tallies approximately with the initiatory legends of the East. There is no need to be more precise on this front, as nothing that was essential has been altered.

Let us start working. As was said when we began these meetings, before learning anything else, we must put into practice in our daily life everything we know. With the little we have understood of the thought of Jesus, we have centuries of work before us. But this time will pass quickly if, fused into the joy of divine love, we steadfastly consecrate all of our labors and all of our efforts to our Friend.

www.ingramcontent.com/pod-product-compliance
Lightning Source LLC
Chambersburg PA
CBHW020327170426
43200CB00006B/296